*For Marjan, Nidham and Mina*

# DIFFUSION OF TECHNIQUES, GLOBALIZATION AND SUBJECTIVITIES

*With the Compliments of the Author*
*Paris, 9/7/2019*

# DIDIER GAZAGNADOU

# DIFFUSION OF TECHNIQUES, GLOBALIZATION AND SUBJECTIVITIES

ÉDITIONS KIMÉ
2, impasse des Peintres
PARIS IIᵉ

Original title: La diffusion des techniques et les cultures
Kimé, Paris, 2008.

Translation from French  L. Byrne.
Illustration: G. Mina, Quelques couleurs du ciel, 2014.

Editions Kimé, Paris, 2016

ISBN 978-2-84174-741-2

http://editions kime.fr

# FOREWORD TO THE ENGLISH EDITION

The publication of an English version of this essay brings me immense pleasure and I wish to extend warm thanks to Béatrice Charrié for making it possible, as today, an English translation creates the opportunity for ideas and hypotheses to be read, debated and shared on a very broad scale.

In this essay, I wished to place the question and role of technical diffusions in the process of capitalistic globalization and assess the cultural and subjective effects produced by these diffusions. I also wanted to briefly revisit the theme of diffusionism in the history of anthropology. The study of diffusions has been subject to heated debate in the history of this discipline, leading to the emergence of a diffusionist wave, particularly in Germany and Great Britain. Even if some of these diffusionist authors often exaggerated their hypotheses, they were also frequently too brutally dismissed or even held in contempt, particularly in France, although they raised genuine questions at times. In contrast, in the United States, Franz Boas and his students managed to demonstrate the interest of questions relating to diffusion and borrowing, in spite of widespread criticism of their diffusionist approaches. The beginning of the 21st century confirms – to put it mildly – the importance and the impact of all sorts of diffusion throughout societies around the world and diffusion should thus be an important research domain for contemporary anthropology.

In addition, in order to facilitate the reading of this essay for English-speaking readers, all the citations have been translated into English, while keeping the original references to the French texts.

Finally, I wish to address special thanks to my friend and anthropologist colleague Daniel Terrolle for taking the time to read this essay and for his very useful comments and criticisms.

Paris, 19 October 2015

"Myths, tales, currency, commerce, the arts, techniques, tools, languages, words, scientific knowledge, literary forms and ideals, all that travels, is borrowed and in a word does not result from the history of a given society. There is thus reason to ask what this unequal coefficient of expansion and internationalization depends on."

*Theories de la civilisation*
Marcel Mauss
Œuvres, volume 2
1974 : 454.

# INTRODUCTION

Today, the idea that cultural globalization entails mixing and the reinvention of traditions is dominant[1]. This is incontestable, but it is imperative to add that this mixing and reinvention only make up a moment of the contemporary globalization phase. Globalization is a historical process of long duration, linked to developments and to the diffusion of techniques, particularly transport and communication techniques, since the first human migrations. Therefore, mixing and reinvention only account for a moment in this major transformation and do not describe a much more profound process: that of the complete transformation of all cultures and the setting up of subjective movements shared by more and more sets of individuals throughout the world.

This historical movement is mainly linked to the progressive and generalized diffusion of techniques, and to the worldwide diffusion of the same techno-scientific and industrial system since the 19th and 20th centuries. It is imperative to analyze this process from its starting point in Eurasia over at least the past 10,000 years.

The role of techniques and their diffusion in the different globalization phases must be anchored in the depths of human history, in the same way as the general diffusion of a particular subjectivation issued from a given cultural area, regardless of the different mixes and achievements (*"bricolages"*) of local cultures.

It turns out that in the history of anthropology, authors known as diffusionists intuitively seized the importance of these movements of technical and cultural diffusion during the 19th and 20th centuries. But "diffusionism" was not, and is not popular today – unlike theories of mixing, reinvention and acculturation[2] – even though it raised a series of questions reiterating contemporary problems. It is thus important to discuss the manner in which anthropology tackled and problematized diffusions.

The Eurasian zone played a preponderant role in the history of techniques and their diffusion and is thus decisive in the history of globalization. In particular, the diffusion of techniques in Eurasia and the amplitude and the cultural effects of this diffusion raise vital issues. The Eurasian zone is a privileged zone since, as André Leroi-Gourhan wrote; "a fact emerges from archaeology: at the beginning of historic times, the main techniques are confined to proportionally limited geographic areas, following an axis crossing temperate Eurasia. This by no means resolves problems concerning origins, but raises the question of technical diffusion" (Leroi-Gourhan 1973: 303-304).

We will take account of examples of diffusion in very different cultures and cultural zones, at diverse historical periods and in various geographical areas. But, we will also focus on problems associated with the phenomena of non-borrowing or the refusal to borrow which raise as many questions as borrowings, and we will integrate these into the general diffusion process.

Within this vast Eurasian zone, Middle East societies, including those from the Muslim period, were the interface between eastern Asia (China, the Asian steppes and India) and Europe (Italy, Spain) and will thus serve as focal points. Our key areas are sedentary and nomadic societies in the Middle East as well as the Muslim civilization. This is partly due to our experience and specialization in these areas, but also because this geographic and cultural zone appears to raise certain fundamental issues central to this work: the diffusion of techniques, borrowing and non-borrowing and their impact on pre-modern and contemporary societies. However, we will also take examples from other societies.

All these questions are rooted in extended timescales and, from an anthropological viewpoint, are designed around questions related to the contemporary world. The impact of techniques is a fundamental question for which there are two main points of view: either techniques and technical systems are considered to be crucial in the history of societies; or on the other hand they are considered to be determined by the political and cultural choices of social actors.

One of the aims of this essay consists in reevaluating the effect of the diffusion of techniques on cultures, and, to analyze cultural and subjective developments in the current phase of globalization. Our perspective is based on Leroi-Gourhan's hypothesis that some techniques are more determining than others (Leroi-Gourhan 1971: 35-42), and forces us to approach the question of the global orientation of societies and contemporary cultures as a result of the diffusion and setting up of a common techno-economic system.

We stated that globalization is not a new phenomenon but a long-term process: we will thus embark on a journey from prehistory to contemporary times; through China, Iran, the Middle East (and the Maghreb[3]) or Europe.

Eurasia is an immense geographic and civilizational area consisting of powerful states and powerful societies of nomadic pastoralists (Briant 1982), stretching from Japan to the British Isles. It is worth repeating that this geographical entity plays a specific historic role. On one hand, all the human groups from Eurasia were in contact with each other at one time or another and borrowed quantities of cultural and technical elements from each other. On the other hand, for geographical, ecological, natural and technical reasons (Leroi-Gourhan 1973: 311-313), fundamental inventions were to emerge from Eurasia, leading humanity, in the very long-term, towards a "modern" and contemporary world.

Indeed, from around the 10th millennium B.C. and during a long and slow historical and technical process, Eurasia was to be the land of invention and diffusion of determining technical facts; namely: the domestication of plants and cereals, animal domestication, agriculture, metallurgy, wheeled vehicles, writing, gunpowder, paper, etc.[4]. Obviously, this does not signify that societies from other continents did not create or invent anything: they all participated in the elaboration of human civilization, but at different times and with different effects: let us recall the invention of the first lithic tools by societies in Africa and the diffusion of this technology throughout the rest of the world. Societies outside Eurasia were confronted with two main problems; their relative isolation on one hand, and the fact that they only disposed of part of the elements, materials, minerals, plants, and animals, on the other hand, which collectively would have been conducive to new developments.

Many anthropologists, historians and archaeologists have exposed, in their way and in their domain, the central role and the advantages of the Eurasian zone for world history.

André Leroi-Gourhan rightly underlines the importance of the geographical factor for Eurasia in writing: "their geographical position put men from south of the forests in a marked state of superiority: the savannah and the steppes host grasses, equids, camelids and bovids" (Leroi-Gourhan 1973: 319).

In this way, being on the Eurasian axis meant being better situated than others since "the best grounds bear the best equipped" or inversely, "the best equipped occupy the best grounds" (Leroi-Gourhan 1973: 316). Leroi-Gourhan was not insinuating with these formulae an absolute determinism of the environment, but the obvious fact that societies installed in an area with "domesticable animals"[5], minerals, cereals, forests, grazing ground, water, etc., were potentially in a very favourable situation. These societies are, in any event, in a more favourable situation than ethnic groups who only dispose of some of these elements to constitute new techno-economic and political designs. The distribution of the main technical themes for each civilization, established by Leroi-Gourhan, illustrates this important environmental determinism (Leroi-Gourhan 1973: 326). The geographical factor provides the possibility of more varied and complex techno-economic combinations; Leroi-Gourhan writes: "we are thus led to consider a well circumscribed geographical environment [Eurasian axis] as the basis of superior forms of technical progress" (Leroi-Gourhan 1973: 313)[6]. From this ecological and technical viewpoint, the best geographically located human groups, i.e., those with access to abundant and varied minerals, plants and animals, were the Eurasians: Nomads, like the Iranians from the steppes, Turks and Mongols from central Asia and Upper Asia, sedentary and nomadic Arabs from the Middle East, sedentary peoples from China and Europe or societies combining sedentary and pastoralist civilizations such as in the Middle East. Whatever the case, these different social organizations have established links with each other since ancient times (Briant 1982).

The essential traits of our civilization were fashioned in this geographic zone, from the 2nd millennium at the latest: "agriculture, livestock farming and metallurgy make up the basis of technical activity and until the 20th century, everything results from the consequences of the symbiosis of the three technical groups of farmers, breeders and smiths" (Leroi-Gourhan 1973: 313).

We have chosen to examine the crossroads of different civilizations, to highlight the Middle East cultural areas which repeatedly create networks and links with eastern Asia and Europe due to extensive nomadic activity (Arab, Turk then Mongol), especially from the 7th century onwards. The Muslim civilization was probably, after the Neolithic and before the Turk-Mongol expansion, one of the major phases of globalization. It is apparent that this line of thought falls within the scope of anthropology, but also encounters questions relating to history, geography, archaeology and economy.

In this essay, we wish to grasp and to expose the importance of technical then cultural diffusions, by reactivating some of the questions raised by "diffusionists". We run the risk of pushing our interpretations a little too far in a "diffusionist" direction! This is for us the meaning of an essay: ongoing work in which we aim to develop problems and raise questions and where inevitably, it will always be possible to underline lacunae, even errors, as well as the hypothetical nature of certain ideas. This said, although we are in partial disagreement with Claude Lévi-Strauss in his criticism of diffusionists; we share his very true and up-to-date point of view concerning the frame of mind of the latters' adversaries:

"Anthropologists from the diffusionist school of thought did not think twice, [...], about forcing the hand of historic criticism. I do not wish to defend their adventurous hypotheses; but it must be said that the attitude of their cautious adversaries is just as unsatisfactory as their opposite line of fabulous pretentions. [...] *To deny the facts, because one believes them to be incomprehensible, is certainly more sterile from the point of view of progress and knowledge, than to elaborate hypotheses; even if they are inadmissible, and precisely because of their shortfalls, they give rise to criticism and research which help to overtake them*" (Levi-Strauss 1958 I: 272-273).

This essay thus aims to reexamine these questions, some of which were raised over a century ago, from the anthropologists interested by diffusions. Uunfortunately, these questions have been neglected by most anthropologists. Here, we will look at techniques, the industrial technical system and their diffusion on a global scale because the link between the diffusions of techniques and the massive transformations of cultures and subjectivities are very clear today.

# I. A FEW WORDS ABOUT DIFFUSIONNIST ANTHROPOLOGY

Anthropology has generally been dominated by evolutionism from its beginnings, as much so in the United States as in Europe. The discovery of new societies with or without a State, organized according to very different principles from European societies, raises many questions. One of the main issues stems from the difference in technical and industrial development between European, American and societies from other continents. How can we explain these differences? Are they due to isolation and the absence of contacts? Or rather to internal logic? Do these societies represent what all societies once were? The question of contacts between civilizations was raised at an early stage – by Henri Lewis Morgan and Edward Burnett Tylor – and was only partially explored. Diffusion and borrowing were identified in relation to cultural traits, techniques, art, languages, etc. This led to controversy and heated debate, to such an extent that a new branch of thought, called diffusionist, and came into being towards the end of the 19th century and especially at the beginning of the 20th century[1]. But let us focus for a moment on the question of evolution.

The evolutionary orientation of anthropology, like that of a lot of 19th century thought, is rooted in life sciences (zoology, comparative anatomy), and namely in embryology and research into development and evolution. In fact, from the 18th century onwards, the question of the development of the animal embryo was the subject of much research and discussion. The rupture came towards the middle of the 18th century, when Wolff advanced – in his study of the formation of the chicken's intestine – the thesis of leaf-like layer formation as opposed to the previous theory of preformation which backed up the idea that everything was already preformed in the egg (Canguilhem & alt. 1962: 19-26; Dupont-Schmitt 2004: 7-9). During the 19th century, embryology continued to develop, mainly through the work of Von Baer, considered to be the founding father of modern embryology (Canguilhem idem: 41-47). The knowledge acquired concerning the development and the evolution of the embryo was so important that it influenced, contaminated and oriented the historic, archaeological and sociological sciences of scholars such as Comte, Boucher de Perthes, Spencer and of course Darwin (Canguilhem idem: 49-78). Like the other "humanities", anthropology assimilated the idea of evolution, emphasizing notions of evolutionary stages and sub stages. Anthropology referred to as diffusionist thus adds the concept of diffusion to the idea of evolution. Indeed, during the 19th century, the concept of diffusion was not always opposed to that of evolution. The polemic between Adolf Bastian (the founder of German anthropology) and Friedrich Ratzel (the founder of anthropogeography) illustrates this point. Ratzel advocates the idea of the transformation of societies through diffusion and thus through borrowing ideas, objects and techniques, from a center of inventions. Bastian, on the other hand, while accepting diffusion facts places the emphasis on internal dynamics. This does not prevent these two authors, like others, from associating cases of diffusion with an evolutionary interpretation: as evolutionary stages were surmounted by societies through contacts and borrowing. Diffusion phenomena do not just refer to internal and vertical cultural dynamics but also to transversal dynamics and of course to the general idea of transition and integration of an element or a trait from one culture to another, or to several others. The concept of borrowing, which is obviously linked to that of diffusion, refers to the concrete process of integration of one or several elements into one or more given cultures.

Given this major evolution-diffusion division, it is appropriate to add nuances, particularly as far as German ethnology and anthropogeography are concerned, but also for evolutionary authors such as E. B. Tylor or H. L. Morgan. Effectively, these authors, and particularly Tylor, did not in any way deny the role of borrowing in the evolution of societies.

In any event, the question of diffusion was so omnipresent that certain anthropologists decided to create a viewpoint opposed to that of the evolutionists, to be qualified as diffusionist. Broadly speaking, the question of diffusion, which had raised so many discussions, almost completely disappeared from the field of anthropology, and even though cases of diffusionism are indicated, the issue remains marginal. This question has even been completely rejected. In order to understand why the question of diffusionism immediately became a controversial theme in anthropology, to grasp the reasons behind its disappearance and renewed interest in the subject, we will present a brief but not exhaustive overview of the question, based on a number of representative authors.

In the perspective of a reevaluation of this diffusionist question and the ensuing debates, we will refer to some of the works of Franz Boas in the United States and his "students", such as Alfred Louis Kroeber, Clark Wissler, Alexander Goldenweiser and Edward Sapir. For Great Britain, we will retain certain works of W. H. R. Rivers, Grafton Elliot-Smith, W. James Perry and Pitt-Rivers and for France, those of Gabriel Tarde, Paul Rivet and George Montandon. In the domain of German anthropology, we will make reference to Friedrich Ratzel, Léo Frobenius and Father Wilhelm Schmidt, all interested in the question of diffusions. Although Mauss, Leroi-Gourhan, Haudricourt and J. Needham cannot be categorized among the diffusionists, they will be cited as they contributed to reflections on the general question of diffusion and techniques. All of these authors, in varying degrees, carried out research on cases of diffusion, then, with the exception of the folklorists in France, Germany and Austria (Niederer 1987; Bausinger 1993), the diffusion issue progressively fell into disuse.

From our point of view, it is André Leroi-Gourhan from the middle of the 20th century onwards, who completely renewed the approach to the diffusion question with the concept of *technical tendency*. However, in the second half of the 20th century, Joseph Needham's research on the diffusion of certain techniques and Chinese scientific knowledge towards the Muslim world and Europe (Needham 1954) could have and should have reopened the debate on the question and the role of diffusion in Eurasia. Yet, this only very partially transpired and mainly among the historians of China. In the same way, André-Georges Haudricourt (1966, 1987) studied several cases of diffusion of techniques although they were not a central part of his work, and using mainly linguistics drew up methodological and heuristic problems. However, this did not incite anthropology to reexamine the diffusion question. Among historians, it is important to mention the work of Marc Bloch who underlined the importance of this issue in Eurasia early on (Bloch 1983c, 1983d). Then Fernand Braudel pointed out the major role of borrowing by Europe (Braudel 1979 I, II, III). Generally speaking, archaeologists are the only ones who appear to have consistently expressed real interest in diffusion and continue to do so (Guilaine 2005; Vigne 2004; Cauvin 1997). But, no more than at earlier stages, these new openings and orientations were not to be followed by major developments in anthropology.

Rather disparate authors, theories and viewpoints are often classified in the category of *diffusionism*. For example, while G. W. Stocking Jr. designates W. H. R. Rivers as *diffusionist* and identifies him as the founding figure of this branch in Great Britain, the same author employs the term *neo-diffusionist* to characterize the work of G. Elliot Smith, W. J. Perry and A. M. Hocart. It is thus a little hasty to categorize certain authors in specific branches, as according to the same Stocking, part of Rivers' work is totally evolutionary (Stocking 1996: 179-232). Rivers himself, after having criticized the Graebner method, writes that his own work on Melanesia is anchored between a certain relevant treatment of evolutionism and that of historical schools – "The general mode of treatment of this book holds a middle course between those of the evolutionary and historical schools..." (Rivers 1914). At the same time he affirms that contacts between peoples and the ensuing mixes are factors of human progress (Rivers 1914 II: chap. XV, 1-8). It is clear that the diffusionist category is relatively subjective, let us say rather elastic. This is confirmed by the point of view of Herskovits who identifies three schools of thought – English, German-Austrian and American – "who founded their study of cultural history problems, culture dynamics or both on diffusion phenomena" (Herskovits 1967: 197). But Herskovits does not follow exactly the same classification as Stocking and does not generally label authors as diffusionists. For his part, Robert Cresswell designates F. Ratzel as the father of the diffusionist school, while admitting that his position is less radical than that of his disciples (Cresswell 1975 1: 13).

Strictly speaking, only anthropologists with theories affirming that diffusion alone is a determining factor in the constitution and transformation of societies should be branded as diffusionists. In other words, those who consider that a first invention is always issued from a cultural area and then diffused and borrowed from other societies; leaving little room for independent inventions. Yet, when we look closely, anthropologists adhering to these theories are few and far between, if not inexistent.

In reality, the diffusionist category simply refers to authors who emphasize diffusion phenomena, as opposed to evolutionism, with more or less successful results. This is the case for certain ethnological work, such as that of Grafton Elliot Smith or William James Perry, treated as hyperdiffusionist by Lowie. These authors accord a decisive role to all kinds of diffusion in the constitution of human cultures, and at times, they reach rather exaggerated conclusions (in the case of W. J. Perry). But even in their case, we cannot rigorously extrapolate this viewpoint to all of their work.

### DIFFUSION IN THE GERMAN ANTHROPOLOGY TRADITION

German anthropology is the product of different epistemological traditions and is strongly influenced by medicine, natural sciences and the work of geographers like Berlin Humbolt and Ritter (Trautmann-Waller 2004). In 1869, Bastian, the veritable founder of German anthropology, published an authentic anthropology review with Hartmann: the *Zeitschrift für Ethnologie*. This review backed up the theory of ideas and elementary thought, marking a rupture with previous publications. These ideas are fundamental ideas found in different places throughout the world with their own cultural characteristics, such as tools, arms, religion (Fiedermutz-Laun 2004: 61-76). Bastian began to argue with Ratzel, in particular against his interpretations in terms of diffusion (Fiedermutz-Laun 2004: 69). For Annemarie Fiedermutz-Laun, "the conflict opposing Bastian and the anthropogeographer F. Ratzel (...) essentially concerns whether, when analogies arise, we can envisage the

possibility of parallel development or that of the diffusion of a civilization". (Fiedermutz-Laun idem: 70).

Although German anthropology is evolutionary in substance, like
all of the 19th century, it is nonetheless sensitive to these notions of diffusion and elementary ideas. This entails a paradox: on one hand, the
idea of the genius of each people develops from the end of the 18th century onwards, namely through the work of Herder. Each people has a
specific spirit - *volkgeist* –, which encompasses a singular character and
a specific culture (Herder 1991: 99, 104, 155). On the other hand, the
idea that diffusion and borrowing-imitation are processes underlying
different nations (Herder idem: 158-164) is also present, particularly
in Herder's work. The 19th century German tradition retained these two
themes, influenced by Herder (Dumont 1983: 115-120). The notion of
elementary ideas is present in Bastian's work (Fiedermutz-Laun 2004;
Bausinger 1993: 48) and the idea of diffusion is clearly manifest in the
work of Ratzel, Graebner, Frobenius and Schmidt who, each in their
own way, adapt the theory of elementary ideas coupled with the idea
of diffusion to evolutionism (Fiedermutz-Laun 2004). This theory pos-
tulates that simple ideas (such as believing in ghosts) are present in all
humans and in all societies (psychic unit of humanity), but the limits
of human inventiveness explain the diffusion of inventions in a given
place and their propagation through cultural circles (*kulturkreise*). The
historical approach is of the utmost importance for these German authors and Wilhelm Schmidt is insistent on this point:

*"In Germany, the honour of the historic reaction is due to Fried-*
*rich Ratzel. He affirms the historical character of all peoples and the*
*necessity of studying the historic events of their past, especially their*
*migrations [...]. His disciple Léo Frobenius based his theory of "cir-*
*cles" or cultural areas on Ratzel's doctrine. [...] Graebner and Anker-*
*mann restudied the problem."* (Schmidt 1931: 278-281).

As with all authors categorized as "diffusionists", caution must
also be applied to the German authors. Take, for example, Leo Frobenius' *Histoire de la civilization africaine* (1952), which raises questions
of diffusion between Asia, the Middle East and Africa (Frobenius 1952:
166-211), and which does not appear to be systematically diffusionist
(idem 1st part: 11-40). Moreover, the extent of ethnographic documen-

tation is impressive. In a similar fashion, in one of A. Bastian's rare texts translated into French concerning Central American sculptures, there are no diffusionist theories apart from an allusion to incontestable migrations within the Americas. This text consists rather of a classical, cautious and erudite ethnographic analysis of Guatemalan stone sculptures (Bastian 1887: 264-305).

## DIFFUSION IN ENGLISH AND AMERICAN ANTHROPOLOGICAL TRADITIONS

In opposition to evolutionary theory and adopting the widespread 19th century idea concerning the limited nature of human inventive abilities, Elliot Smith focuses on the thesis of the diffusion of beliefs, religious ideals, ritual behaviour, habits, decorative symbols, lifestyles and behaviour, architecture, etc. In order to back up his theories, Elliot Smith cites the example of the expansion of Muslim civilization and the colossal diffusion of knowledge and cultural traits that this entailed, an example which irrefutably represents a solid argument from a diffusionist perspective (Elliot Smith 1933: 33-35). But Elliot Smith is interested in diffusion because of a more theoretical issue. He questions the reasons why so many ethnologists put so much energy into denying diffusion phenomena (Elliot Smith 1933: 2), a fundamental question which we will expand upon below. Notwithstanding this, it is difficult to deny that Elliot Smith was prone to excess at times, namely with his theory on the diffusion of "heliolithic" culture[2], which would have spread from Egypt towards Africa, Europe and Asia and finally attained the Americas (Elliot Smith 1929: 14, 37, 133). Moreover, it is mainly because of this theory that Elliot Smith is systematically classified a diffusionist (Lowie 1971: 147; Mercier 1966: 106) and that most of his research is disregarded. Adam Kuper's recent book on the history of British anthropology – which is incidentally very interesting – emphasizes the caution of the functionalists as opposed to the implausible theories of Elliot Smith and Perry (Kuper 2000: 11-14). Kuper even denies the fact that Elliot Smith wished to resign from the Royal Anthropological Institute, to protest against the censoring of his work[3] (Kuper 2000: 13). However, Elliot Smith's work on the history of Muslim civilization and the major ensuing diffusion, or on the diffusion of religions such as Buddhism or Christianity, remains valid today and does not warrant so much irony. The diffusion and the influence of the Muslim world on Europe are attested in the domains of science, medicine and techniques; in the same way as the influence of Buddhism on the Chinese Medieval economy (Gernet 1956) or that of Christianity on South America, for example.

For his part, William James Perry, also impassioned by ancient Egypt, which he considered to be the departure point for much cultural diffusion, does not reject the notion of independent invention and thus the originality of cultures. He simply recalls that in any event an original idea or an invention is not born *ex nihilo*, it is often the product of borrowing, which combined in a certain way, leads to innovation. He cites the example of relationships between the Greeks, the ancient Middle East and Egypt (but there are others) to back up his hypothesis (Perry 1935: chap. XXIII).

It is more surprising to see authors such as Franz Boas and his students Clark Wissler, Edward Sapir, Alfred-Louis Kroeber and Alexander Goldenweiser, categorized as diffusionists, as this does not transpire from their texts. In a particularly polemical article, Leslie A. White (1945: 335-356) largely accuses all these anthropologists of getting waylaid in diffusionist interpretations, rejects their criticisms of evolutionism, emphasizing the fact that Morgan and Tylor had already widely underlined the importance of diffusionism in the makeup of civilizations. L. A. White's aim in this article consisted mainly of legitimizing his own technological evolutionism. Although these authors accorded a certain importance to diffusion and borrowing as dynamic factors in relations between societies as well as in their internal development, none of them ever advanced a diffusionist theory of culture and societies.

The founder of American anthropology, Franz Boas, had a very marked influence on anthropology in general. He was interested in linguistic and mythological diffusion in Indian societies and took part in this controversy. It is important to recall that he studied science and anthropology in Germany and was one of Bastian's students. It is undoubtedly for this reason that he was categorized as a diffusionist, despite evidence to the contrary. Indeed in a famous article called *"Evolution or diffusion?"* (Boas 1924), Boas engages in a critical analysis of

both evolutionary and diffusionist theories. Boas provides the methodological basis for understanding possible diffusion phenomena, retain-
ing three ethno-historic conditions:

*Firstly*: the anteriority of the object or cultural trait compared to
the more recent object being studied must be proven.

*Secondly*: it must be proven that the more recent element really
derives from the older one.

*Thirdly*: it must be established that dynamic conditions increase
from periphery towards the centre, in other words, it must be possible
to observe intermediary types between the most recent and the oldest.

Arguing against evolutionism and Tylor in particular, Boas rejects
the theory of the survival of older elements as proof of an older phase
and of the transition from one socio-historic stage to another. The simple
fact that Boas noted cases of diffusion and borrowing between Indian
tribes based on ethnographic observations, does not in any way ratify
categorizing him in the diffusionist rank. Moreover, Margaret Mead
recounts that Boas considered as early as the 1920s that "enough had
been shown of populations borrowing from each other, that no society
developed in isolation, that each society was continually influenced by
other peoples, other cultures and other techniques" (Mead 1977: 127).

Similarly, in Clark Wissler's work, we encounter criticism of alleg-
edly diffusionist authors, such as Graebner, Rivers or Elliot Smith, just
as we find criticism of those who advocate the systematic independence
of inventions (Wissler 1923: 102; 1927: 99-106). With regard to diffusion, Wissler bases his argument on different cultural and technical facts
spread by diffusion, such as the horse or corn (Wissler 1923: 111, 121).
In order to refine our understanding of the phenomena and diffusion
processes, he forges the concept of natural diffusion, which indicates a
process of involuntary diffusion, and that of organized diffusion characteristic of a deliberately propagated project from one culture to another,
like in the evangelical missions during colonial periods or conquests (id.
1923: 129, 159). But while he closely follows cases of diffusionism,
Wissler is always careful not to lapse into certain "diffusionist" analyses
(Wissler 1923: 102). In his *Histoire des Indiens d'Amérique du Nord*,
Wissler exposes the considerable and dramatic consequences for Indian
societies of the introduction and the diffusion of what he calls "the three

strange presents of the white man" to American societies: the gun, the horse and alcohol (Wissler 1969: chap. XVIII). These three cases represent natural diffusion in Wissler's sense of the term, but his analysis does not stop there. He shows that borrowing the gun is an important fact in itself but that what this borrowing brought about is much more complex. In this case, the Indians were confronted with two technical problems that they never resolved, firstly repairing damaged guns, a technique that they never mastered, and secondly with the problem of gunpowder, that they never learnt how to make. The borrowing of this instrument thus left them in a position of inferiority and dependence. Moreover, borrowing the horse radically transformed their lifestyles. Some Indian groups became nomads, and all of them became more mobile, notably in horse combats against Europeans. However, this never compensated their long-term military inferiority[4] due to the fact that they could not produce gunpowder. As for alcohol, it was just a social, psychological and cultural disaster for Indian societies on the whole[5]. Wissler's analyses are simply anthropological rather than diffusionist.

Alexander Goldenweiser was interested in the same diffusion phenomena as Boas. In a collective work focusing on diffusion, he affirms that for him, diffusionism was just a method that cannot be systematically used. This prompted him to write: *"a sufficiently large number of cases will remain where no safe or even tentative conclusion can be reached between diffusion and independent invention. And, in honesty and fairness, this also must be admitted"* (Goldenweiser 1927: 99-106). For him, invention and diffusion are two fundamental and very widespread processes (Goldenweiser 1937: 465). Furthermore, Goldenweiser underlines the selective aspect of all borrowing; a selection linked to the risk of transformation of cultural habits (idem: 484).

An author like Edward Sapir who develops a theory of linguistic borrowing, based on fieldwork and study of the Amerindian languages, can by no means be classified among the diffusionists (Sapir 1967). The fact that he was interested in the manner and the rules by which words are transferred – or not – from one Amerindian language to another does not by any means imply that these languages were only formed by diffusion. Sapir proposes linguistic borrowing rules founded on what he calls morphological and phonetic evidence (idem 1916-1967: 277-

281). An understanding of the structure and phonetics of the languages of two populations in contact with each other makes it possible to identify whether certain words – referring to certain practices or techniques – are borrowed. Effectively, each language has its own characteristics and discriminations, and when certain words are borrowed from another language, these words are invariably transformed. For example, the "p" in Persian was very often transformed into a "b" in Arabic, which obviously does not mean that every Arabic word containing a "b" is of Persian origin; it is imperative to analyze the root, the morphological structure and to refer to comparative semantics. The case of the "Arabic" word *funduq* which means hotel today, but which signified in medieval Islam a place to store merchandise, to rest and to carry out transactions, is suitable for a "Sapirian" type analysis. The Arabic language is made up mainly of triliteral roots although there are also some quadriliteral Arabic roots. It is thus this quadriliteral structure of the root (*funduq* = *fa/na/da/qa*) which drew our attention and prompted us to identify the non-Arabic origin of *funduq,* which is incidentally Byzantine (Gazagnadou 1986a). This shows that Sapir's method for discerning borrowings between different societies can be exploited in a pertinent manner. André-Georges Haudricourt also underlined the importance of the analysis of words and their historic etymology when he studied the diffusion of the technique of iron smelting in Eurasia (Haudricourt 1987), although Haudricourt does not by any means belong to a diffusionist tradition.

Sapir was conscious of the dangers of a perspective systematically focused on diffusion issues when he wrote "the interest in diffusion facts and the historic deductions that they entail, has eclipsed phenomena of convergence [i.e., of independent inventions]; and even gone as far as denying them" (Sapir 1967: 149).

Alfred Louis Kroeber wrote an important article on the question of diffusion in which he advanced the concepts of *stimulus diffusion* or *diffusion by stimulation, controlled diffusion* and *diffusion by contact* (Kroeber 1940). When he evokes stimulus diffusion, Kroeber refers to a situation where it is not the element itself or the technique which is diffused, but simply the idea; the stimulation in this sense refers to the desire to reproduce or recreate what was observed. He cites the case of the "invention" of the fabrication of porcelain in Europe at the beginning of the 18th century. Chinese porcelain had been imported into Europe for the past two centuries and was widely appreciated. This attraction and high importation costs incited Europeans to produce this type of object themselves and therefore to discover the technique. It is in this way that after a long period of experimentation and research, German chemists discovered kaolin and managed to develop specific techniques in 1708-1709 leading to the development of a technique of porcelain fabrication. On a superficial level, this discovery appears to be an independent or parallel invention whereas it is not. Europeans were in contact with Chinese objects and although there was no borrowing or transfer of Chinese techniques in the strict sense of the term, for Kroeber, this is a case of stimulation. On the other hand, the case of the technique of paper manufacture is to be ranked in the category of diffusion by contact as we can almost follow the path of this technique from China to Italy through the Muslim world (Carter 1925). Controlled diffusion refers to cases where the borrower selects part of a technique or a cultural complex.

The concept of stimulus diffusion directly influenced Joseph Needham in the way he perceived diffusion problems from China towards the West, that is to say, towards the Muslim world and Europe (Needham 1954). In our point of view, Needham overused this concept to argue in favour of technical or scientific diffusion from China towards the West, whereas we do not dispose of accurate elements proving that such diffusion actually occurred. There is a clear difference between the porcelain reinvented in Europe from the Chinese model of imported Chinese vases and the cases evoked by Needham, such as the compass, the rear rudder, the wheelbarrow, which are cases of diffusion by direct contact, for which the exact path, and even the diffusion itself, has not yet been clearly established.

## DIFFUSION IN THE FRENCH ANTHROPOLOGICAL TRADITION

In France, there was no real interest in diffusion issues. The long forgotten late 19th century works of the sociologist Gabriel Tarde were revived by Gilles Deleuze in the 60s and 70s and deserve a mention

(Deleuze 1968: 38-39). Tarde was not defined as a diffusionist, nor did he participate in anthropological debates on the subject, but his theory of imitation and counter-imitation is similar to diffusionist theories on a social level. We could even say that Tarde's theses enriched diffusionist schemes. Tarde advanced an original interpretation of societies in terms of imitation and counter-imitation, borrowing or refusal to borrow, which gave rise to heated debate with Durkheim[6]. Tarde wrote: "At the beginning of societies, the art of knapping flint, domesticating the dog, fashioning bows, later making bread, working bronze, extracting iron, etc., must have spread contagiously, each arrow, each piece of bread, each bronze fibula, each knapped flint was both a copy and a model" (Tarde 1890: 19). For Tarde, there are two forms of imitation, either copying the model, or doing the opposite (Tarde 1890: Preface). The individual, considered as an entity of desires and beliefs, either mimics or counter mimics others. This amounts to diffusion in successive waves and transforms individuals and societies (Tarde 1890). On the other hand, Durkheim believes that social transformations take place through the coercion applied by abstract collective representations (Durkheim 1986: 4-12). Thus, interaction between individuals and groups – in Tarde's work, there are only individuals caught up in networks – leads to relationships between societies. For Tarde, human societies from prehistoric times onwards, borrow quantities of elements and objects, which explains why they share and transform common traits (Tarde 1890: 56-57). It is interesting to note that Tarde had a certain influence on Boas (Stocking 1974: 31, 101, 239) and the American school, but virtually none on the French tradition dominated by Durkheim's theories.

Still in the domain of French anthropology, the ethnologist Georges Montandon, who read Graebner and was influenced by the theory of diffusion circles, elaborated a theory called "cultural ologenesis", which claims to be a global theory of the formation of life, the evolution of societies and a treaty of cultural ethnology. This theory is often considered to be diffusionist although Montandon underlined the methodological aspect of this perspective: "The main process of progress in civilization is thus diffusion [...]. We observe that this is above all a method. The diffusionist method, as opposed to other methods, [...]

encourages research into distribution and geographic precision for an element or a set of elements. This method is freed from looking for causes, but at the same time does not abandon or eliminate them, it merely advances hypotheses and leaves a lot to be done by prehistorians" (Montandon 1934: 31-32). Montandon's methodological caution concerning this question is noteworthy; but only on this question, since as everyone knows, he did not display the same caution in the political sphere, serving the Vichy government during the Second World War[7].

Paul Rivet is also one of the rare French ethnologists to become involved in diffusion questions, while denouncing the dangers of this branch (Rivet: 1929, 1930, 1939). We can cite, for example, his comparative linguistic work on Sumerian and Oceanian languages or his study of gold working and its diffusion in America. Generally speaking, Rivet was interested in diffusion facts, but never excluded the possibility of a parallel invention. Moreover, like Leroi-Gourhan at a later date, he emphasized the importance of ethnology for studying techniques as "they last for longer than the conditions" (Rivet: 1929). Once again, it is clear that it is important to reevaluate the categorization of each author as diffusionist.

### ABOUT DIFFUSION AND DIFFUSIONISM

Lastly, it appears that these diffusion debates can be reduced to two essential theoretical problems:

*Firstly*: the question concerns the causes of the transformation of human society and thereby of the links between history and anthropology. Evans-Pritchard resumed this point well, by stressing the role of history in the interpretation of the evolution (meaning transformation) of societies and the links between these societies. Evans-Pritchard shared Kroeber's (excessive) viewpoint, considering that anthropology in the United States was fundamentally "characterized by an anti-historic tendency"; and showed that functionalists had seized the opportunity to reject all historic perspective by attacking evolutionists and diffusionists for some of their historic rhetoric (Evans-Pritchard 1974: 49-51). Moreover, this debate surrounding the history of anthropology is still ongoing, as Jean-Luc Jamard (Jamard 1993: 221-241) recently pointed out. In order to demonstrate the necessity of tempering arguments, let us cite the case of Malinowski. In his book entitled "*Une théorie scientifique de la culture*" (1968), Malinowski is clearly opposed to the historic approach to culture – which is logical for a functionalist -, but admits the importance of diffusion facts, especially in contemporary times (1968: 175-183). Then, in "*Les dynamiques de l'évolution culturelle*" (1970), Malinowski fully accepts the fact that the diffusion of extrinsic models radically modifies societies. He takes the example of the European colonization of Africa, where diffusion entails a major transformation of African societies. It is important to recall that Malinowski has quite a balanced viewpoint of authors referred to as diffusionists in his presentation of anthropological theories (Malinowski 1968: 18-35).

*Secondly*: the diffusion and borrowing between social groups and between societies attested by anthropologists and historians are so important that it is difficult to discern exactly what characterizes the identity of a culture, just as it is difficult to explain the different developments in societies. To fully accept diffusion facts is in contradiction with two of the themes central to 19th century thought until the beginning of the 20th century: the idea of evolution and of evolutionary stages and therefore of more evolved societies than others and that of the nature of the identity of Europe. There are countless diffusion facts and cultural traits but is not easy to establish any kind of proof of their existence. As we have seen, many different authors refused to deny the reality of diffusion facts and tried to establish them whenever possible, in opposition to radical evolutionism. This is the often polemical context in which diffusionism emerged and it is legitimate to ask, after reviewing the matter, exactly what reality this category corresponds to. In fact, this category refers to authors and works that point out the importance of diffusion facts and try to retrace their pathways and the moment at which borrowing occurs, whereas most anthropologists concentrated on the analysis of a given society on its own. Lastly, the category of diffusionism was above all a polemical category used in the history of anthropology to settle scores with its adversaries.

To conclude on the question of the denomination and the use of the term diffusion, we can perhaps coin the term diffusionist for some of the work of Elliot Smith and Perry for example, as they incontestably went too far in the diffusion hypothesis without concrete and accurate arguments. But, we can neither reject nor spurn all of their research and even some of their hypotheses. Unfortunately and as often occurs in "academic" circles, the easiest way to dismiss a problem is to disqualify it. In this way a whole series of English, American and German anthropologists were categorized as diffusionists merely because they showed an interest in studying diffusion facts.

Diffusionism existed in some cases (but more rarely than it seems) when authors exaggerated the role of diffusion in the formation of cultures. But in each case, as we have shown, different distinctions are required. It is for this reason that we pay tribute to those German, English, American and a few French anthropologists - often with other specialties – who through their observations, studies and research on the diffusion of cultural, artistic and technical traits contributed as much to our knowledge of civilizations as the better known authors still categorized as evolutionary and functionalist. Today, diffusionist anthropology, as school, no longer exists because of all the hostility aimed at this branch throughout time, but the question of diffusions remains. Therefore, if "diffusionist" refers to an approach aiming to highlight and analyze diffusion facts, then this term seems perfectly acceptable.

It was the work of André Leroi-Gourhan that led to renewed interest in the diffusion question. His research on techniques resulted in rethinking and advancing issues related to invention and diffusion.

## II. THE DIFFUSION OF TECHNIQUES

The question of the technique *per se* has been the subject countless works and will not be reiterated here. However, before tackling the problem of the diffusion of techniques, it is relevant to briefly recall some important points.

In the history of anthropology, the question of technique and techniques was brought to the fore in France, more than elsewhere. Marcel Mauss considered this as an essential focus of ethnology, and even advanced the idea that the technique in the 20th century had replaced the economy as a determining factor in the transformation of societies (Mauss 1969 (1938) T.3: 249). Then André-Georges Haudricourt, who was close to Mauss, also focused on this field of research. But André Leroi-Gourhan was the only scholar to examine the technique at its root, a subject we will develop below.

Anthropology progressively moved away from the technical question which became little more than a compulsory, but secondary aspect of all ethnological studies. In France, although the anthropology of techniques had always occupied a non-negligible role, following the reflections of the three previously cited authors, technique was still not accorded the important role it deserved in anthropology. Robert Cresswell rightly and severely criticized the fact that anthropologists had practically abandoned research in technology[1]. The study of techniques was subjected to different terminology: technology, comparative technology, anthropology of techniques or even cultural technology; whatever the denomination, it was, in all cases an anthropological approach to the technique and its connections with a human group and sociopolitical and economic structures. This lack of interest is astounding as technique is an essential aspect of all social organization, whatever the cultural area and historic period. In France, in line with the research in technology conducted by Mauss, Leroi-Gourhan and Haudricourt, a certain number of anthropologists[2] continued to focus on techniques, mainly in the aim of grasping an object or a technical process or its integration mode in a new technical system.

Developing Mauss' reflections on techniques, Leroi-Gourhan created a theoretical system based on techniques, from his prehistoric and ethnological fieldwork. These writings still provide today some of the most stimulating reflections on the subject. As for the historians, the names of Marc Bloch (1983), Maurice Daumas (Daumas 1962-1979) and Bertrand Gille (1978) are famous for having instigated developments on the research of techniques. In Germany, in the field of ethnology (*Volkskunde*), diffusion problems were mainly raised through research on popular cultures, before collapsing into the abyss of national-socialist fascism like a lot of German language sciences. In Great Britain, following the works of Malinowski and Radcliffe-Brown, the functionalist current dominated anthropology and the issues of diffusion and the diffusion of techniques were no longer addressed. The names of Elliot-Smith and Perry were scorned and the focus was on the internal analysis of societies and on the notions of structures, functions and needs. In the United States, following the work of Boas and his influence on his students, diffusion phenomena were taken into consideration in a more general framework, particularly for the study of Indian cultures, but there was no focus on techniques. Anthropologists and historians in the United States illustrated their interest in techniques in the review "Technology and culture". But in the Anglo-American world, technique historians concentrated mainly on the history of innovation and particularly during the industrial period (Edgerton 1998). On the other hand and generally speaking, it is worth repeating that archaeology and prehistory were very attentive to the diffusion of techniques, especially for the Neolithic period. These disciplines based their theories on tangible material discoveries and brought to light the slow but incontestable diffusion of various techniques (agricultural, domestication, fabrication, etc.) from the Middle East towards other Eurasian regions.

### FOR A WIDER DEFINITION AND A NEW CLASSIFICATION OF TECHNIQUES

We will retain the definitions of technique advanced by Mauss, Haudricourt and Leroi-Gourhan: an effective action on matter, a milieu or the body, through the mediation of a human body, instruments, tools and machines.

However, we suggest widening this definition, so that the technique becomes: an effective action on a mineral, vegetal, animal or individual (technique of the body and intellectual technology) environment or on a population (technique of power). The latter is a political technique aimed at controlling a population or social groups. We will reconsider this question in the next chapter with a specific example.

In addition, it seems necessary to reassess the hierarchy of techniques developed and advanced by Leroi-Gourhan. Having classified the elementary actions on matter, Leroi-Gourhan proceeded to categorize techniques into three categories: acquisition techniques, fabrication techniques and consumer techniques. Up until this point, we are in agreement with this classification. But, when he tackles the question of transport, and after writing "transport synthesizes forces and ensures the means of reaching raw materials and of diffusing products" (Leroi-Gourhan 1971: 19), Leroi-Gourhan places transport - wrongly in our view - in the category of acquisition techniques.

Indeed, how can the first elementary actions be applied to matter if no transport and communication techniques exist in the first place (signals, noises, language[3])? In all situations, Man must first communicate and travel (from the smallest to the largest space), in order to indicate, for hunting for example, the route of a troop of animals, to be able to localize food and transport materials. There is an inextricable link between transport, communication and mobility. Mobility is a characteristic of human beings. For Joseph Reichholf "[human] locomotion and its constant progression opened up increasingly vaster spaces and countless new possibilities of existence" (Reichholf 1994: 222). Then, much later on followed the domestication of the horse, the dromedary, the camel and the donkey, which increased social group mobility and transport capacities.

The mobility of individuals and groups led to the elaboration of transport techniques, which form the basis of acquisitions, transformation of societies, contacts and exchanges between social groups and societies. Their presence, their absence, their speed or their slowness largely set up, organize and determine the future of all societies. It is possible to possess a rich and complex mythology but without means and techniques of transport, all human groups find themselves in difficulty at one moment or another. From the Palaeolithic to the present day, the problem remains the same.

That is why techniques of transport and communication should, in our opinion, take their full place alongside acquisition, fabrication and consumer techniques; thereby modifying the classification of Leroi-Gourhan.

Technique did not play a central role in anthropology, notably for premodern and traditional techniques. It is true that recently there has been more focus on contemporary techniques, generally called technologies. But, there is a question which has been almost totally neglected by anthropology and technology, *namely the diffusion of techniques*.

## THE DIFFUSION OF TECHNIQUES

We have seen that the study of diffusion in anthropology in general during the 19th century and the first half of the 20th century thwarted the will of many anthropologists and historians whose objective was to formulate a global theory of the evolution of societies by establishing a hierarchy between these different societies.

This question of evolution was prevalent in biological sciences (Taylor 1992: 269-271) long before anthropology. The latter is dominated by two postulates; the unity of the human mind on one hand and its limited innovative ability on the other hand. Debates between evolutionists, diffusionists, functionalists and independents (Boas, Mauss) on diffusion in general and techniques in particular were organized around these three elements: the quest for a global theory of evolution, the unity of the human mind and the poor innovation of the mind.

Evolutionists such as Morgan and Tylor focused on techniques in their own rights and on a lesser scale, on their diffusions. Tylor is even sometimes wrongly considered as the instigator of what was later to be called diffusionism.

Morgan's theses on kinship and evolution are widely cited. However, this is not the case for his work on techniques, apart from one exception reported by R. Cresswell (Cresswell 1996: 224-225), or the role of techniques in the transformation of societies and the important role that he accorded to animal domestication, which he considered to be a major technical fact. It is important to emphasize that for Morgan, the invention of the bow and the arrow, pottery, iron working, ceramics, etc., are technical inventions which led to the transition from one stage or substage to another (Morgan 1985: 7-14). For him, techniques of food production are the prerequisite for human migrations across the globe (Morgan 1985: 19). Technical diffusions make up an obvious fact: "Where continental links exist, it seems that each tribe must have taken advantage, to a certain extent, of the progress accomplished by the others. All major inventions and discoveries spread, but lesser advanced tribes must have appreciated their value well before being able to appropriate them." (Morgan 1985: 43).

Moreover, it is noteworthy that for Morgan the absence of contact between societies and therefore of technical diffusions are responsible for the fact that societies remained at a certain level of development; this is the case for example for the North and South American Indians who remained stuck at a certain evolutionary stage (Morgan 1985: 43). This being said and although he cites Tylor (Morgan 1985: 14), Morgan did not develop diffusion questions any further, as we have already mentioned. This is one of the contradictions, or at the very least, a problem from an evolutionary point of view. In effect, how can one explain that all societies do not go through the same stages and that some remain at archaic stages, even though they all have the same intellectual capacities (the unity of the human mind is an evolutionary postulate)? Especially given the fact that evolutionists themselves observe that there was contact at least between some of these societies and that they could thus have borrowed fundamental techniques? Morgan, no more than the other evolutionists, did not provide any answers to this question. It is important to recall the fact that Morgan immediately saw that techniques and their possible diffusions were a fundamental element in the history of societies.

For Tylor, the question was different as his work often focuses on technical diffusions (Tylor 1876: 74-75; 1865: 325). This can be explained by the fact that his research was based on tangible cases: for example the diffusion of the Chinese samovar in Russia (Tylor 1865: 165), or the possible diffusion of the technique of steel production by fusion, from eastern Asia towards Madagascar (Tylor 1865: 167) or again the diffusion of the fork (Tylor idem: 173). The diffusion of techniques is an integral part of Tylor's work on techniques and this is an important factor for understanding the processes underlying the formation of societies (Tylor idem: 360). For Tylor, the question of technical diffusion and inventions is an "important problem" (Tylor 1865: 325) and a major anthropological issue in so far as this question is linked to that of the evolution of the human genus (Tylor 1865: 360).

F. Ratzel, for his part, often prefers diffusion to invention interpretations, particularly in the domain of techniques (Ratzel 1896: I, 80-81; II, 405-436). Ratzel conducted a fascinating study of the diffusion of the bow and the arrow in Africa, in which he presents the distribution of the bow, from the north to the south of Africa. But he also explains that certain warring tribes refused to use the bow and the arrow for a long time as they considered that "all arms designed to be used at a distance are cowards' arms". In this way the Somalis tribe abstained from firearms for a long time (Ratzel 1887: 5). In his *Géographie politique*, intended to be a reflection on the links between state and territory, Ratzel shows the influence of migrations through conquests (of the state or nomadic tribes), for technical and cultural diffusions (Ratzel 1897: 191).

Marcel Mauss occupies a unique position. In effect, Mauss is characterized – like Franz Boas – by the fact that he never developed a global theoretical system, yet he considerably influenced anthropology. He also stands out because he accorded key importance to techniques: for Mauss the technique should be a central preoccupation in anthropology. It is for this reason that he is often presented in France and in the discipline as the initiator of research in ethnology and in the history of techniques. Mauss was indeed among the first to advance a precise definition of technology and technique: *"Technology… rightly claims to study techniques, the whole technical life of Man from the origins of humanity until the present…"* (Mauss 1969 3: 250). As for technique, it is, he pursues, *"a group movement, a generally and mostly manual, organized and traditional action, competing to achieve a known physical, chemical or organic aim."* (Mauss idem 3: 252). Mauss even goes as far as adopting the idea of the primacy of technique in social transformations: *"By nature, techniques tend to be widely used and to multiply in all peoples. They are the most important factors among the causes, the means and the ends of what we call civilization, and also of social and human progress"* (Mauss idem 3: 197). Having participated in all the debates, Mauss also partook in the debate between evolutionists and "diffusionists". If techniques as such, were part of his reasoning, the question of the diffusion of techniques and cultural traits did not elude him. The borrowing of elements between civilizations is an essential fact which must allow for the understanding of the formation process of different societies (Mauss idem 3: 614-616). And according to him, we should be able to retrace the paths of certain diffusions, albeit with caution. In a chapter devoted to civilizations dating to 1929 (Mauss 2: 456-472), Mauss tackles the question of the essential role of technical diffusions. He thus defends the idea that diffusions and borrowings play a non-negligible role on the orientation of culture in countless circumstances.

André-Georges Haudricourt, following the line of some of the work of Mauss, oriented his research towards cultural linguistics and technology. In this context, he became interested in very different domains, namely cases of technological or scientific diffusions from China towards Europe and vocabulary diffusions. On a methodological level, Haudricourt imposes conditions for studying diffusions, notably in *"L'homme et la charrue à travers le monde"* (Haudricourt-Delamarre 1986), in his work on the origin of modern plough teams (1936 and 1945), on the origin of the car (1948) or on the origin of iron smelting (1952). As well as the technological study, Haudricourt believed it necessary to study vocabulary and the words used to designate techniques in different cultures (Haudricourt 1987: 51-56). However, although Haudricourt was interested in diffusion, it would be absurd to categorize him as a diffusionist.

## ANDRÉ LEROI-GOURHAN AND THE DIFFUSION OF TECHNIQUES

A. Leroi-Gourhan's approach to problems of diffusion and invention is a veritable innovation and a real turning point. In effect, Leroi-Gourhan created a new concept: the technical tendency. He defines the technical tendency as "an inevitable, predictable, rectilinear characteristic; it incites the handheld flint to acquire a haft, the bundle dragged by two poles to obtain wheels [...] The wheel entails the emergence of the crank, the belt drive, transmission" (Leroi-Gourhan 1943: 27). The technical tendency or technical virtuality runs through the interior milieu (all of the intellectual and cognitive baggage of a group) of all human groups, but in order to materialize it must find ways of manifesting itself through technical expressions: "We see the technical tendency as a movement in the interior milieu, of a progressive hold on the exterior milieu. This movement is not affected by systematic divisions, we cannot conceive a classification of tendencies, as these only become explicit once they are materialized and then cease to be tendencies" (Leroi-Gourhan 1945: 336). Leroi-Gouhran borrowed this concept from Bergson, who probably owes it to embryology. In *L'évolution créatrice*, Bergson repeatedly employs the notion of *"tendance"* (*tendency*), which, for him, seems to be a characteristic of life and the process of evolution and the transition from the cellular world to the plant, animal and human world (Bergson 1941 (1907): chap. II). But more importantly, in certain passages of *l'Evolution créatrice*, the notions of forms, of elementary states and of *homo-faber* appear. In Bergson's work, the notion of tendency refers to the idea of virtuality which can only become real in a movement of materializing (Deleuze 1968: chap. V). The materializing of this virtuality depends on a certain number of conditions.

Given the abundant references to zoology and life sciences, Bergson probably borrowed this idea from a particular phase of embryology concerning the development of the embryo. This development consists of three main phases: growth, differentiation and determination. All embryos possess a set of virtualities; an embryo will only definitely become what it is to become from the determination phase onwards; up until that phase, other orientations remain possible (cf. *Joseph Needham* in Gazagnadou 1991: 67). Bergson then shifts this question into the general perspective of a theory of evolution and writes: "the biologist who practices geometry, easily triumphs over our inability to give an accurate and general definition to individuality. A perfect definition only applies to an existing reality: yet vital properties are never fully accomplished, but always in the process of being accomplished; these are tendencies rather than states. And a tendency only obtains everything it aspires to if it is not hampered by any other tendency..." (Bergson 1941 (1907): 12-13).

The Bergsonian perspective thus gave Leroi-Gourhan, encouraged by his research in prehistoric technology, the possibility to definitively leave behind the false debate between invention and diffusion, by creating the concept of "*tendance technique*" ("technical tendency"). Technical tendencies go through all "interior milieus", which is to say in all societies, and aspire to find favorable conditions in the "exterior milieu" (made up of animals, plants, minerals and people from the same region), in which to transpire. This allowed Leroi-Gourhan to explain the appearance of the same tool in regions and cultures which never has the least contact with each other, like the example of the different types of ploughs. Although Leroi-Gourhan senses that the tendency implies local invention and diffusion, he only contemplates this implication in terms of results, that is to say through materialization (Leroi-Gourhan 1943: 28). In this respect, from our point of view he remains trapped in a narrow vision of technical tendency. It appears to us that technical tendency implies invention and diffusion, even as virtuality – and not only in materialization phases. The technical tendency itself contains two possible manifestation modes: one consists of immediate materialization or (technical) invention (linked to immediate favorable conditions); the other consists in deferred materialization or (technical) diffusion because it is hampered by immediate unfavorable conditions. The technical tendency (or technical virtuality) has an irreversible character because technique, up to a certain point, is biologically rooted. This idea is advocated by Leroi-Gourhan and applied to the relationships which form during the course of human evolution between the brain, the hand and the tool (Leroi-Gourhan 1964 and 1965). The works of the biologist and zoologist J. Reichholf (1991: chap. 12 and 13) are in accordance with some of Leroi-Gouhran's hypotheses. However, these questions are still subject to debate. For some paleoanthropologists, the relationship between upright posture, the evolution of the brain, the freeing of the hands and the use of tools, still raise questions. Lastly, the concept of technical tendency raises the question of the uniqueness of the technical tendency or rather its multiple character. In our point of view, there is a fundamental technical tendency (which aims to have a real effect on milieus and materials) which consists of several technical tendencies and diverse technical realities in the process of being materialized.

That being said, although the concept of technical tendency in Leroi-

Gouhran's work is founded on a certain evolutionary determinism in the technological field, it was never based on an absolute determinism, especially in the ethnical domain: "These peoples are no more primitive than us" (Leroi-Gourhan 1943: 16). There is a similar idea with a different formulation in the work of Claude Lévi-Strauss, who, while recognizing the objective and current techno-scientific superiority of Europe, wrote: "We can be sure that if the industrial revolution had not first appeared in western and northern Europe, it would have taken place one day somewhere else on the globe" (Lévi-Strauss 1952: 65).

Historians such as M. Bloch, F. Braudel, M. Lombard or R. Bonnaud, also attributed a significant role to diffusion phenomena in historic processes, but these issues were not met with much enthusiasm; a little more in recent decades, it is true. In the ethno-technological sphere and the remarkable research of A-G. Haudricourt, we have just seen that interest for technical diffusions remained limited.

In 1954, Needham raised the question again for a series of techniques which appeared to him to be of Chinese origin. But for him, this was just a minor aspect of his work on Chinese sciences and techniques. It is probably for this reason that he confined himself to the concept of stimulus diffusion advanced by Kroeber. The concept of stimulus diffusion raised real issues which prompted the technique historian B. Gille to cast doubt on a number of diffusion hypotheses advanced by Needham and Haudricourt (Gille 1978: 441-443).

In the domain of agriculture, archaeologists and historians brought to light early on the fact that the fundamental agricultural and livestock techniques from the Neolithic period were diffused and borrowed by numerous other social formations in Eurasia.

It is even more surprising that the question of the diffusion of techniques remained marginal and neglected given that anthropologists and technique historians were constantly confronted with the diffusion of techniques and different forms of borrowing with more or less sophisticated levels of integration. Techniques and their diffusion have rapid implication for all societies, cultures and even cultural areas throughout human history.

It is true, and this is worth repeating, that the study of diffusion phenomena raises real identification problems. It is not always easy to find and present proof (sources and/or materials) and elements. For the diffusion of techniques, the object, the tool, the machine make it possible to retrace the geography of the diffusion, even when the technical object or the technique is perfectly integrated.

What is striking is the resistance – both conscious and unconscious – of anthropologists in accepting the hypothesis of the importance of technical diffusions and their influences on cultures. This situation is beginning to change under the weight of reality. The stakes are both theoretical and political: advancing possible or probable borrowing as the first heuristic hypothesis clearly disturbs our perspective on cultures. Effectively, in the analysis of the construction of cultures, emphasis is either placed on the homogeneous or the heterogeneous; in other words, either on internal logic or on borrowing. Moreover, the diffusion of techniques insistently raises the question of technological determinism and the social capacity of control on what generates and entails a technique or a technical system. These considerations do not in any way exclude non-diffusionist research, approaches or hypotheses, as parallel invention can never be excluded.

It is also necessary to take account of the cases where diffusion/borrowing do not materialize, or the "refusal to borrow", as Fernand Braudel calls it (Braudel 1969: 293-296). The study of cases of non-borrowing is for us an integral part of the anthropological approach to diffusion. Indeed, these cases reveal and raise various questions which shed light on the internal and external dynamics of societies in contact with each other.

## TECHNOLOGICAL AGNOSIA

In order to characterize these cases of non-borrowing and based on some of our studies, we suggest using the term *agnosia*, which is a concept borrowed from cognitive sciences. The concept of agnosia refers to experiences where the subject only perceives part of a situation, cancelling out the other elements (Buser 1998: chap. X). Indeed, the phenomenon of technical non-borrowing probably takes complex psychocultural processes into consideration, resulting in human groups missing out on the effective advantages of borrowing. We will refer to such cases as *technological agnosia*.

The study of cases of diffusion and borrowing regularly reveals situations where borrowing does not materialize in spite of a favourable context. We will concentrate on technique here as cases of non-borrowing raise a whole new series of questions and namely the most important for comparative technology, central to Leroi-Gourhan's work: how is it possible to explain non-borrowing when the object or technical instrument in question is undeniably more effective than that used by the neighbouring group? The question is also significant from the point of view of the concept of technical tendency.

For Leroi-Gourhan, the fact that a human group does not borrow a given tool from a given neighbouring group has three possible explanations: either because the potential borrowing group is in a state of technical plenitude; either because there is a very significant technological gap between the two groups; or lastly because the group does not feel the need to adopt the tool in question (due to technical superiority, technical inertia and technical plenitude Leroi-Gourhan 1973: 375). We can accept Leroi-Gourhan's viewpoint, but for us, the notions that he uses do not allow us to fully understand cases of non-borrowing, especially if we conserve his concept of technical tendency, as we do. Indeed, as Leroi-Gourhan points out "the only traits transmissible by borrowing are those which improve processes" (Leroi-Gourhan 1945: 304), which means that they are superior. Therefore, how can we explain certain cases of non-borrowing which would have brought an irrefutable improvement? This raises the question of what Braudel referred to as "the refusal to borrow". But the notion of refusal does not seem satisfactory as it does not increase our understanding of the phenomenon. For this reason, we wish to borrow and use – with caution – the work of cognitivist approaches and Gregory Bateson's "eco-anthropology," which sheds light on this problem. We will illustrate this point using three technical cases.

*Three examples of technological agnosia: the cart, the wheelbarrow, the stirrup*

The wheel - and the techniques deriving from the wheel – is a question rightly considered by Mauss as being of the utmost importance (Mauss 1967: 81). Generally speaking, transport and communications are central to technology. J. R. Forbes pointed out in 1955 in *Studies in ancient technology* (Forbes 1993: vol.2: chap. 3 and 4) that the use of wheeled vehicles (tanks, carts, chariots) was progressively replaced in the Middle East by transport using pack animals (mules, camels, dromedaries, donkeys, horses). This question is extremely important for technology and the economy and was reassessed by R. Bulliet (1978). According to Bulliet, the prevalence of pack animal transport as opposed to the use of wheeled vehicles is principally economic. He considered that as the financial cost of pack animal transport was lower, the development of wheeled vehicles was marginalized. We consider this viewpoint to be too limited and we propose a very different hypothesis, which nevertheless includes Bulliet's hypotheses. Indeed, it is essential to take account of the political context and in particular of the complex and conflicting relations between the main nomadic tribes and the central Middle East powers ([4]). The political and military power of these major nomadic tribes (Turkish, Iranian, Arabic) rivalled with the central powers of the regions in consideration and kept them at bay (Bonte 1987; Digard 1987; Gokalp 1987; De Planhol 1968). These permanent conflicting relations clearly prevented the construction of a strong, centralized and territorialized state, capable of building a network of roads for wheeled vehicles. Thus, the prevalence of pack animals at the expense of towed vehicles continued after Muslim expansion until the 20th century. The technological agnosia or non-borrowing of the cart, from the Turks to the Mongols, thus has a political origin in this case (Gazagnadou 1999).

*The wheelbarrow*

The history of the wheelbarrow is just as problematic. B. Gille categorized the wheelbarrow with the minor issues (Gille 1983), whereas it seem to us to reveal a much wider problem for cultural technology as this "minor issue" refers to the major and general issue of the history of wheeled vehicles in the Middle East. This small wheeled vehicle operated by a single man and used for transporting matter and small materials was invented in China (Gernet 2003: 128; Needham 1954: 258-281) in the 1st century. Then the wheelbarrow (with one or two wheels) appeared in Europe towards the end of the 13th century. It is for the time being impossible to determine whether it represents a parallel invention or a case of diffusion from China to Europe. The existence of contacts between the Muslim Middle East and China is attested from the 8th to the 9th centuries onwards. Although most of these cases represent contact between traders and travellers, there are also cases of contact between Muslim and Chinese scholars (Gazagnadou 2001b), especially during the Mongol period. Travellers and traders must have seen wheelbarrows in the very active Chinese towns. Moreover, later on, in the 13th century, the wheelbarrow probably appeared in the Middle East during Mongol army invasions, in the presence of Chinese technicians and engineers who were familiar with the advantages of the wheelbarrow in military campaign logistics.

However, the wheelbarrow only appeared in Egypt at the very end of the 18th century, following the French invasion (Jabarti 1965). Thus, the wheelbarrow ([5]), this small, simple and technologically unsophisticated vehicle was hardly used in the Middle East, until the 20th century (Gazagnadou 2007). What explanation can account for this phenomenon? The structure of the economic system and the availability of cheap labour must surely have played a role but this explanation does not appear to be sufficient. Can the nature of the technical system of Pre-Modern Muslim civilization explain this case? Perhaps, but it is still poorly known. We still do not have answers concerning the case of the late diffusion of the wheelbarrow.

## The stirrup

The history of the invention and the diffusion of stirrups in Eurasia is also a very interesting case. The long accepted famous thesis of Lynn White Jr. (1962), considered stirrups to be a Chinese invention, ignored by the Sassanid Persian cavalry, introduced to Iran by the Arabic-Muslim cavalry, who borrowed them from Central Asian Turks when crossing Iran (White 1962). From our point of view, White's interpretation can no longer be retained today (Gazagnadou 2001a). Archaeologists discovered the oldest stirrups in Mongolia (1st-2nd centuries B.C.), several centuries before they appeared in China. This was thus a case of a nomad invention followed by diffusion from the steppes towards the

Chinese world and the Middle East. Moreover, our reexamination of a famous Iranian bas-relief (*Taq-e Bustan*) and the discovery of new elements in Arab sources ignored by White allows us to advance the idea that stirrups were known to the Sassanid cavalry and were adopted at the very end of the 6th century or during the first quarter of the 7th century, at the latest during the reign of Khosrau II (591-628). Then, during the conquest of Persia, the Arab-Muslim cavalry, who didn't use stirrups, borrowed them and diffused them rapidly towards the West (Gazagnadou 2001a). Although our thesis is different from that of White, an important problem subsists: that of the non-borrowing of stirrups from Turkish nomads by the Sassanid cavalry. The Sassanids had a long history of regular contact, conflicts and alliances with the Turks for several centuries and were thus perfectly familiar with the equipment of Turkish mounts. Lastly, stirrups are small, easy to make technical objects which are advantageous during fights on horseback when cavaliers wield heavy weapons. One possible hypothesis can be advanced: mounting with stirrups could initially have been perceived as a dishonour by state army cavaliers and may thus have been a way of differentiating nomad cavaliers. However, we must admit that this question remains open.

## TECHNOLOGICAL AGNOSIA, DIFFUSION AND TECHNICAL TENDENCY

It is imperative to relate these cases of technological agnosia to Leroi-Gourhan's reflection on technical invention which evoked "mental acts by which technical intention leads to the materialization of a new, perfected object, [mental acts which] are the associations", the latter being "at the origin of all progress" (Leroi-Gourhan 1945: 397). Technological agnosia is for us a psychological and cultural phenomenon which does not amass all the necessary associations for addressing and evaluating the contribution (in terms of efficiency and esthetics) which could result from borrowing a given technique or cultural trait.

However, we wish to underline the fact that mounts with stirrups were diffused throughout the whole of Eurasia from the 8th century onwards, then throughout the entire world. In the same way, for wheeled vehicles, the diffusion of the cart with a mobile front axle and the wheelbarrow occurred in the Middle East and in the Muslim world from the end of the 19th century and during the 20th century (Gazag-nadou 1999 a; Mohebbi 1996).

In the case of wheeled vehicles, the deferred materialization of the tendency towards automobile vehicles is, for Leroi-Gourhan, a very early technical tendency (Leroi-Gourhan 1973: 343). The diffusion of the wheelbarrow is part of the general movement of diffusion of wheeled vehicles. In the case of stirrups, it is a universal deferred mate-rialization of a physical tendency seeking increased stability.

Thus deferred materialization (or diffusion) continues to render the concept of technical tendency pertinent. These examples show that the concept of technical tendency, as we have already mentioned, in-cludes both diffusion and invention.

"Invention" describes the moment when a tendency becomes im-mediately materialized, in other words, the first time that conditions are favourable in the exterior and technical environment of a human group.

Diffusion describes temporally deferred materialization, due to resistance from the exterior environment at a historic moment for a human group. It is in this way that wheeled vehicles spread from the Middle East in the 20th century, as this globalization phase of industrial technical systems made it possible.

Although it is possible to observe deferred materialization of the technical tendency by studying a given technique, it remains difficult to explain these cases of agnosia and an ethno-technological or political interpretation alone is insufficient. It is imperative to add a cognitive ap-proach. Sander Van der Leeuw advances an interesting point concern-ing the cognitive dimension of links between men and techniques after studying Mexican potters. According to him, the evolution of the human cognitive system goes through fast, complex phases which play a deci-sive role in the conceptualization of space, for example. He also pos-tulates that the speed of Neolithic technical innovations is the result of new cognitive development (Van Der Leeuw 1994a: 38-41 and 1994b: 311-328). For his part, Basalla imputes an important role to dreams and fantasy in the development of technology (Basalla 1988: chap. III).

For our part, we wish to focus on the issue of the perception and the organization of time from a cognitive point of view. It is possible that this aspect, along with the technopolitical factor, played a major role in the non-diffusion of wheeled vehicles in the Middle East: the advantage of these vehicles being masked by the fact that the perceptive system was designed around pack animals.

All cultures form cognitive frameworks which structure members' perception and orient their actions in a certain direction, in order to maintain a balance between these frameworks and the social complex they belong to. Gregory Bateson demonstrates this in his work on the Iatmul (Bateson 1971: chap. 13) and Balinese (1977: 120-139) cultures. Diffusion leading to borrowing a technical element or cultural trait can destabilize the cultural and political frameworks of the borrowing group. Let us take the example for the contemporary period of the borrowing of Anglo-American music (*Rock n'roll* or *Rapp*) by traditional societies in Indonesia and Iran. In both these cases, this borrowing immediately had destabilizing political repercussions in that state powers or society were more or less violently opposed to these new types of music ([6]). In the same way technical borrowing can destabilize the technical-cultural structure of whole societies, as was the case with the introduction of steel axes and machetes which participated in modifying the socio-economic structure of the Baruya in New Guinea (Godelier 1996: 361-370). Bateson's work advances the idea of symmetrical relations (Bateson 1977: 77-102). We can apply this concept, generally linked to psychological and cultural situations, to anthropology and technological diffusion and imagine that a refusal to borrow must stem from a refusal to resemble the group in possession of the technique. This idea is similar to the concept of counter-imitation, developed a long time ago by G. Tarde (Tarde 1890).

Phenomena of technological agnosia are even more complicated to grasp in terms of their origin and their function. But one of these functions certainly consists in maintaining a stable techno-cultural state, which explains, as Bateson repeatedly demonstrates, that all societies possess homeostatic systems which aim to conserve internal and external balance (Bateson 1996: 166-184). The concept of agnosia (nonborrowing) used in the technical field, could also be employed in other fields, cultural, economic, etc. The anthropology of diffusion could thus generally refer to anthropological agnosia.

In order to conclude on the question of technological agnosia, we wish to point out once again, that phenomena of technological agnosia only occurred from prehistoric times up until the 20th century. From the 20th century onwards, with the worldwide extension of the industrial technical system associated with capitalism, the whole complex of techniques spread across the entire planet.

However, beyond the debate raised by diffusion, technical non-diffusion and the concept of technical tendency, we believe that the categories of the East and the West, active categories from the beginning of the emergence of European thought, widely contributed to marginalizing diffusion research.

## III. THE CONCEPT OF DIFFUSION AGAINST THE EAST AND WEST CATEGORIES

All the questions addressed must be linked to each other in specific geographic areas in Eurasia. The works of Needham, Haudricourt and Carter on the diffusion of sciences and techniques from China towards Europe oriented our research, as we mentioned above, towards the cultural area of the Muslim Middle East. Indeed, their works clearly show that the weak point of case studies of diffusion from China towards the West is the Middle East. Studies concentrating on China, due to the wealth and diversity of documentation (written, iconographic, numismatic sources, seals, etc.) generally allow us to establish the fact that a given technique or element dates to such a period and even locate the place of invention. In Europe, although there are less sources than in China, we can also sometimes locate the source of an invention, if it is an independent invention; and even the moment at which it arrives in Europe, if it is a case of diffusion (Needham 1954; Gernet 2000, Bloch 1983, Haudricourt 1987). But proof of diffusion pathways between Asia and Europe is not easy to establish. Indeed, as soon as we broach the Arab or Iranian Middle East, studies become difficult due to the lack of detailed sources and a lot remains to be done in order to follow the propagation of a given technique or cultural trait, even where known elements plead in favour of diffusion. Questions subsist in the case of diffusion of the technique of paper fabrication although it has been virtually proven (Carter 1925), but the questions of the diffusion of the compass and gunpowder, for example, remain largely unanswered.

However, these difficulties alone do not explain the lack of work on the diffusion of techniques and cultural traits in the Middle East and

Eurasia. The ideological orientation underlying numerous works in Europe also played a role, particular in the use of the notions of *East* and *West*. We insist on this point, as this division played – and still plays – a crucial role in the structuration of the imagination and studies of non-European societies in Eurasia.

The civilizations central to our work and reflection have long been referred to as "eastern" and "western". This basic division is inacceptable, both to anthropology and history. Indeed, although there are cultural zones and civilizations, each social formation must be individually analyzed. Jack Goody (Goody 1999) criticizes the use of binary categories in all the "visions of the world" (Goody 1999: 16-17). We are going to develop the reasons underlying this *East-West* division.

It is essential to review the whole history of European thought in order to understand the force behind this pair of notions. It is interesting to investigate the history of the formation process of the *East-West* notions, and the implied division. This *East/West* couple has a quasi-warring function in globalization today: in substance those from the *East* (which covers an area including China, the Indian subcontinent, Mauritania and the Middle East!([1])) resist democracy and even a market economy, unlike *Westerners*. We merge here with Aristotle, with just one difference; Aristotle was writing during the 4th century B.C.!

This *East/West* binarism is simplistic and overshadows thought processes and can only really be overcome by the revelation of diffusion facts, which is a task for diffusion anthropology.

### THE EAST-WEST DIVIDE: FROM THE "DESPOTIC EAST" TO THE "DEMOCRATIC WEST"…

The *East/West* divide goes back as far as Aristotle. It is indeed in *Politics* that Aristotle lays down the basis of this divide in writing: "[…] there is another form of monarchy; to which kingships of certain barbarian peoples belong, for example. All are quite similar to hereditary tyrannies subject to law, as barbarians naturally have a more servile character than Greeks, Asians than Europeans, they endure despotic power without complaining […] The former govern, subject to law, consenting [people], the latter non-consenting [people], in such a way that some of them have a guard among the citizens and the others, against the citizens." (Aristotle 1993, III, 14, 1285-a: 257-258). This despotic Asia/ democratic Greece division was to be transformed into the despotic East and the democratic West and was reiterated, in more or less sophisticated ways, by the whole European intellectual tradition until the 19th or even the 20th century. In this tradition, the despotic East mainly referred to Indian, Chinese, Arabic, Ottoman, Persian, Turk or Mongol social formations. The traits attributed to this *despotic East* are echoed with variants and in a scattered way by all the authors after Aristotle, for example, Bernier, Montesquieu or Hegel (Anderson 1978), and are condensed in Marx's analyses. These characteristics are mainly: a despotic political power; an absence of private land ownership, autarkic village communities, a law organized by religion, a powerful bureaucracy with an appropriation of community overworking; state policies on major public works, in particular irrigation, a network of several large towns dominated by the authorities; the annuitant and administrative aspect of towns being generally limited to China.

This tradition and this perception of "eastern" societies, from Aristotle to Marx, operate with the binary East/West structure, in the political, economic, social and religious domains. As Claude Lévi-Strauss writes, this binary vision consists of, on one hand "an older attitude, and which [...] consists of purely and simply repudiating cultural, moral, religious, social, esthetic forms which are furthest from those with which we identify" (Lévi-Strauss 1961: 19), and on the other hand, by the fact that [Greek] Antiquity included everything which was not part of Greek culture (then Greek-Roman) under the name barbarian; western civilization then used the term savage in the same way" (Lévi-Strauss 1961: 20). This type of binary division is present in most societies, however different they are, from China where from ancient times onwards anything that was not Chinese was categorized as barbarian (Gernet 1994: 143-154), or to quote Lévi-Strauss again "in many so called primitive populations who designate themselves by a term signifying "Men" (Lévi-Strauss 161: 384). In Claude Lévi-Strauss' interpretations, it does not appear exaggerated to add that armed and religious conflicts which marked relations between Christian Europe and the Muslim world from the 8th century onwards, especially from the time of the Crusades, favoured and vivified the use of the notions of East and West, as did the conflicts in eastern Asia. The period of colonization maintained this division and it is clear today, that *on both sides*, we still successfully uphold it today!

But, whatever the exact basis of these divisions ([2]), historically European societies and their cultures have systematically dominated other societies and therefore, have imposed the notional "East/West" pair and integrated it into their system of representation and theory.

Concepts of eastern despotism and the Asiatic mode of production are repeatedly present in Marx's different texts ([3]), first in a general and abstract way, in order to contemplate the question of relations and differences between social formations called "western" and "eastern". But Marx provides the first global theoretical and rigourous attempt at defining the "East/West" difference. Indeed, he attempts to give a coherent explanation by relating economic, religious and political instances. Referring to reports from administrators in the Indies, to travel relations, in particular François Bernier ([4]), who relates his extraordinary journey through the Ottoman Empire, Persia and Moghul India (Bernier 1981), to the work of A. Smith and Hegel; Marx encounters and inherits the whole European intellectual tradition (Anderson 1978). Yet in Marx's writings there is a constant evolution and hesitation which is reflected in terminological and conceptual variations: *Asian formations, eastern societies, Asian despotism, eastern despotism and Asiatic mode of production*. These variations appear to be the sign of a problem and an ambiguity for Marx: a problem related to the specific weight of religion, politics and the State in certain historic formations in the Middle East and the Far East, and therefore a problem for the analysis of the historic development of these societies.

Marx has the intuition that these different societies follow specific historic processes which must be thought through separately. However, ambiguity remains as Marx does not totally steer away from the 19th century conceptual field (these hesitations are present in his letters to V. Zassoulicht in the 1880s), dominated by the idea of evolution, which is present in all analyses from this century. This evolutionary ambiguity brings Marx to support the implantation of British capitalism in India and the destructuration of the caste system ([5]) and the autarkic rural economy so that a proletariat can form.

In his *Leçons sur la philosophie de l'histoire* (Hegel 1963), Hegel seems, *in appearance*, to have a better grasp than Marx of certain characteristics of non-European societies, and notably the fact that religion can be a crucial factor in the social formations of Asia and the Middle East ([6]). Hegel engages in long analyses based on much wider reading than Marx; on the bureaucracy of ancient China and Confucianism, then on the relation between Vedism, the caste system and the type of State in India, or the history of Persia. In *Leçons sur la philosophie de l'Histoire,* the question of religion and the influence of religion on the State, wherever it may be, is thought out as the logical and historic development of the Mind towards freedom: "These two nations [China and India], it must be said, do not have an ingrained concept of freedom in their essential conscience" (Hegel 1963: 61). Hegel's vision is part of a theological and evolutionary perspective which is that of the Mind, with a historic trajectory consisting of going from darkness towards light, from alienation towards freedom. Non-European religions and cultures are only considered in terms of their degree of evolution, which is inferior compared to Christianity (Hegel 1963: 346). On the other hand, in *Leçons sur l'histoire de la philosophie,* Hegel is totally aligned with the Greek-European tradition: "Orientals, for example, are men, and free in themselves, as they are; however they are not free as they have no conscience of freedom and accept all religious and political despotism. All the difference between Eastern peoples and those where slavery does not exist is that the latter know that they are free and it is up to them to be free" (Hegel 1990, I: 127). In substance, for Hegel, the theoretical formulations on eastern Asian and Middle East societies do not refer to the field of philosophy but to general ideas, mythologies and religion (Hegel 1990), since the fundamental notion missing from these societies is that they know they are free: "China, Persia, Turkey, Asia in general, that is the domain of despotism" (Hegel 1963: 124). Hegel is thus completely aligned with Aristotelian structural logic, with, in addition, the dialectic and the documentation. As for Africa, for Hegel it is a continent with no history and is of little or no interest...

Lastly, it is Marx's conceptual hesitations which remain the most interesting. In any event, Marx's concept of *Asiatic mode of production* cannot be retained, as Marx applied it to very different social formations, such as Chinese, Indian or Arabic-Muslim societies. Various works (for example, Godelier 1974, 1977 I and II, 1978 and 1984; Anderson 1978; Rodinson 1968; Abd al-Malek 1969: 111-113) have shown for a long time that things were a lot more complex and that it was imperative to apply distinctions in Asia, Africa, the Middle East and America. The idea of *State mode of production* is no better as it is still too general. Indeed, in historic social formations such as the Chinese Tang, the Indian Maurya, Mamluk Sultanate or Mongol power in Iran; the State, with the help of a bureaucracy and a more or less powerful religious hierarchy, plays a dominant role in the organization of society and reproduction, but in each case, this role is different. Chinese bureaucracy, for example, has a very different history, structure and relationship with "the world of the spirits" (Balazs 1968; Granet 1981) than the Indian relationship with religion where the caste system and the question of the religious pure-impure dichotomy have a global sociopolitical effect on both State and society (Renou 1981; Kosambi 1970). There are many other examples, such as what was the link between the Chinese social and political structure during the Tang (607-906) and the Umayyad caliphate (660-749). In the same way, a close look at relations between the slightly Arabicized Turkish military elite and Muslim religious power and its political consequences on the Mamluk Sultanate in Egypt and Syria, clearly shows us another rather singular situation (Ayalon 1996). Lastly, for Mongols in Iran, the political military domination of a minority of superficially Islamized nomadic pastors gave rise to a completely new form of power which was both bureaucratic and nomadic at the same time.

It is clear that a specific study of each of these political formations is necessary and that they cannot be reduced to a common concept. Recently, the 1979 Iranian "revolution" confirmed the shortcomings of the Marxist analysis of non-European societies. We clearly saw the difficulty of Marxist and neo-Marxist categories and analyses in grasping the importance of religion. The influence of duodecimal Shiite Islam in the Iranian process and the power of mobilization of religious mosque networks was, either underestimated in comparison with the workers' petrol strike movement, or considered to come from a misleading effect of the superstructure (the religious discourse explaining the class struggle in a deformed way). But, at the same time, it confirmed the need to formulate specific analyses.

This binary *East-West* category, and the derived *despotism-freedom* and *individualism-holism* notions, which, following the Aristotelian schema, drove the main abstract civilizational division, was partially broken by Marx. However, that was not enough to destroy the effects. In order to get rid of this binarism, it was necessary to adopt a new approach.

AGAINST IDEOLOGICAL EAST/WEST BINARISM:
THE STUDY OF DIFFUSIONS OR NEODIFFUSIONIST ANALYSIS

In order to grasp the possible differences between social formations like those of India, China, the Muslim world and Europe, it thus appears that a strict and simple comparison, however detailed and meticulous, is not sufficient, and ultimately leads to nothing more than a juxtaposition of differences and similarities. The use of wide and loose categories such as "East" and "West", contributes to this comparative approach. This overly wide division is present in one of J. Goody's latest books, not only in the title: *The East in the West* (1999), but throughout the whole of the book. The use of these categories by Goody insinuates, whether he meant it or not, that India, China and the Muslim world have something in common which clusters them together in the "East" category, as opposed to the "West". The West is just as general a notion, which may refer to Vikings or to Louis XI's France. Goody's choice is even less comprehensible considering that he regularly employs these two categories to chart his reevaluation project and writes at the same time "[...] research is still confronted by the "binarism" haunting all "world visions": there are always two types of societies [...,] or two worlds, the Old and the New" and further, "Yet it seems to me that there are few, indeed very few contexts in which this type of division is really useful [...]" (Goody 1999: 16-17) (⁷).

This comparative binary method is not satisfactory as it neglects diffusion and borrowing – or at best mentions them fleetingly, like in the case of the diffusion of the technique of paper fabrication or Indian numerals – but it rarely questions the pathways, the amplitude of diffusion and the impact of these borrowings on receiving societies. A certain number of works and our own research on the general question of the diffusion of techniques and cultural traits, particularly in Eurasia, reveal another methodological perspective. This approach appears to us to be more relevant as it allows us to observe in detail the workings, the possible transformations, the type of integration and the cultural characteristics of the societies having borrowed a given technical element or cultural trait; provided that it is possible to follow the diffused element.

## THE DIFFUSION OF A POLITICAL TECHNIQUE IN EURASIA: THE POSTAL RELAY SYSTEM

Jean Sauvaget raised the question of the sudden appearance of the Mamluk postal relays system (*al-barîd*) in 1260-1261 in a remarkable study of horse posts in the Mamluk empire (1250-1516), but left the question unanswered (Sauvaget 1941). It was essential to take account of the fact that different systems of post houses had existed in Eurasia well before the 13th century. This led us to advance the hypothesis that the problem of a diffusion of the Acheamenid postal system towards Egypt and the Roman Empire already existed in Antiquity (Gazagnadou 2013: annex I). Indeed, in the history of antique Acheamenid, Ptolemaic and Roman postal systems, the vocabulary used suggests that the Acheamenid model was the one diffused throughout the Mediterranean world.

For the Mongol period, the diffusion of the postal relays system is quite well established until the Mamluk Empire. Indeed, there is no doubt that the Mongols borrowed from the Chinese postal relays system (*yi*), as attested by Chinese sources. The diffusion to the Middle East and to Russia of this postal relays system by the Khân Mongols – the famous *yâm* Mongol (Gazagnadou 2013) - is attested by Persian (Joveiny 1912, Rashid al-Din Fazollah 1994), Arabic ('Umarî 1988) and European sources (for example Marco Polo 1982), to cite but a few. There is little doubt regarding the borrowing of the Sino-Mongolian institution by the Mamluks, as illustrated by the date of appearance of the postal relays system, the presence of a certain heraldic symbol on the Mamluk post house and of a sovereign postal insignia identical to that used on Mongol relay postal system during combats in Syria and

Palestine between Mongols and Mamluks ([8]). And diffusion towards Europe seems very likely, although we are cautious for the time being as diffusion towards Italy remains to be confirmed by new documents.

In theory, the study of the diffusion of postal relays system demonstrates the inanity and caricatured aspect of Wittfogel's theory, which only renews with the old binary division: the bureaucratic and despotic State in the East and the democratic State in the West. Indeed, the analysis of the diffusion of the postal institution shows that the State reacts tendentiously in the same way, whatever the cultural area, thereby validating the theses of Fernand Braudel. Braudel defends the idea that the tendency of all States is to want to control (space, populations and financial transactions): "Remodelled or even new, the State remains what it always has been, a body of functions, of diverse powers. The main tasks do not vary although the means employed change constantly. The first task of the state is to be obeyed, to monopolize the virtual violence of a given society for its own benefit [...]; Second task: to control economic life directly or indirectly, to organize the circulation of goods, in a lucid fashion or otherwise [...]. Last task: to participate in spiritual life, without which no society would stay standing [...]. Also, to endlessly survey the strong cultural movements which often contest tradition" (Braudel 1979 2: 459-460). On the other hand, Braudel develops an original viewpoint on the relationships between the State and towns, which he calls the two racers. "But each time, [...] there have been two racers, the State, the City. Usually, the State wins and keeps a heavy grip on the City. The miracle with the first major urban centuries is that the city has fully won" (Braudel 1979 1: 450). The State and the city, or more exactly as F. Braudel saw it, the network of cities, that is, the places where there are capital circuits, have always had relationships of rivalry and collaboration, because of the State's tendency to want to control everything and the city's tendency to want to opt out.

The observation and analysis of the diffusion of the postal system also confirms the triple Braudelain distinction between the logic of the State, that of the market and that of capitalism. Effectively, we saw, in any case with the post, that the State wants to control space and populations. We can also observe the same tendencies everywhere for merchant bankers (in towns) to make arrangements with the State or to try and work around the State; through necessary dealing or exchanging. This tripartition is at work in cultural areas as different as China, the Mongol empire, the Mamluk Sultanate, or Italian powers from the 13th-15th centuries or Acheamenid and Roman powers in Antiquity.

It is for this reason that we are employing the concept *tendency* in the way A. Leroi-Gourhan used the term for technique but transferring it here to state and capitalistic logic: state tendency denotes the tendency of all States to seek to control since space is the challenge and capitalistic tendency denotes the tendency for all capitalism to endlessly accumulate capital, the main issue in this case being time. The differences arise from the more or less accentuated difficulties in materializing these tendencies.

The difference between the Chinese, Arabic, Iranian-Mongol and European post appears in the 16th century, when in Europe the State offers paid postal services to individuals. In Europe, like in the other societies in Asia and the Middle East, the postal system was a means of establishing a grid throughout the territory for fiscal, political and military purposes. But when the State offered postal services to individuals, it contributed to the development of the desire to write and to the development of literacy, but also to the desire to write about oneself, and thus contributed to produce an individual-subject, as defined in Europe from the end of the 18th and 19th centuries. Simultaneously, with this ever faster and continuously increasing circulation of writing and information during the 18th and 19th centuries, resistance and dissidence appeared in the fringes of society, namely in the domain of literary, religious and philosophical writings (Darnton 1991). Then through the worldwide diffusion of numerous institutions during the 19th-20th centuries, all societies adopted this State postal model of transporting individual correspondence.

THE MUSLIM CIVILIZATION AND DIFFUSIONS IN EURASIA

In the history of Eurasia, the Muslim civilization played a key role in the process of diffusion of techniques, sciences and cultural traits. This role stems firstly from the geographical position of the Muslim world, located between the two extremities of Eurasia. Muslim expansion quickly brought China, India, Spain and Europe into contact with each other (Cahen 1995; Miquel 1967; De Planhol 1968). This expansion led to the diffusion and the use of the Arabic language by the literate elite throughout the Muslim world, which entailed a circulation of men and knowledge ([9]).

Thus, this civilization not only invented, but transferred scientific and theoretical knowledge from one end of the Eurasian continent to the other. This was essential knowledge which, in hindsight, had incredible consequences once it reached Europe. Take, for example, the well-known technique of paper making, a diffusion process which spanned the 8th to the 13th centuries (Carter, 1925; Hassan et Hill: 1991: 188-190). The cultural and political consequences of the transition from parchment to manuscript were immense. In the field of science, for example, the consequences of the introduction of Indian numerals and numeral position had a huge impact on European mathematics and on the whole history of science in general.

Still in the domain of science, if we take the example of the geometric theory of algebraic equations ([10]), Roshdi Rashed shows that up until about 1630-1635, Descartes was at the same stage as Khayyâm during the 12th century. Descartes' work leapt forward in 1637, with the publication of *Géométrie* (Rashed 1999: introduction). This example demonstrates quite clearly that mathematic thought and creation have a life of their own, although the diffusion hypothesis cannot be excluded ([11]). This also shows that the ankylosis or decline of creation in the Muslim civilization is not a problem linked to thought.

In the financial and economic domains, the use of Indo-Arabian numerals for accounting must be considered as a financial revolution in comparison to the Roman numeral system.

During our research on Arab and Iranian cultural areas, we came across many cases of borrowing. For example, let us take the "Arab" *funduq* which we fleetingly mentioned earlier: the *funduq* was a place where merchants and traders carried out commercial transactions with their merchandise (Gazagnadou 1986a). The traditional theses affirm that the origin of this commercial institution and the name derive from the Greek *pandokéion* (hotels). Yet, there is a Byzantine institution called *fundicus* which was a warehouse watched by state agents through which merchants passed. This institution existed in the Byzantine Empire before Islam. From a functional and linguistic point of view, there is such close proximity between the Byzantine institution and the Arab-Muslim *funduq* that we established the hypothesis of borrowing and diffusion. The *funduq* system then diffused from the Byzantine world throughout the Muslim world, then into medieval Italy, notably Venice where it was known as *fondachi*.

We have also been able to show the direct influence of Mongols from Iran on the Mamluk Sultanate (Gazagnadou, 1986 b, 1987, 1989a) in diplomatic matters. Indeed the cultural affinities between the Turkish qipchakis - Turks from the Black Sea region who were at the origin of the Mamluk Sultanate – and the Mongols are strong, especially with regard to their relationship to the "religious" and the sacred. The Mamluks from Egypt who founded the Sultanate in the middle of the 13th century were from a Black Sea region under Mongol rule at the beginning of the 13th century. Moreover, their islamisation was late and superficial, at least during part of the 13th century. For a long time, the Mamluk elite were culturally and linguistically very close to the Turkish-Mongols of central Asia. This seems to explain the fact that on Mamluk diplomatic documents, the Muslim *basmalla* ([12]) does not appear as a document header but after the Sultan titles, like for the diplomatic documents of the Mongols from Iran, which is contrary to the whole tradition of Muslim chancelleries (Gazagnadou, 1986 b). This new position of the *basmalla* on Muslim documents is a Mamluk and Mongol chancellery innovation imposed by the not very Arabicised, superficially islamised Sultans and Khâns (Gazagnadou 1994), still close to ancestral Turkish-Mongol nomadic steppe traditions governed by respect for the Khân or Qaghan (heads of clans or tribes).

From the point of view of diffusions on Eurasian networks, the Mongol period, during which a series of powers outside China derive from the Muslim area (Mongols from Iran and Irak), is the most important after the Arab-Muslim period. It is the last (the Timurid conquest did not have the same consequences) and the decisive political pulsation of nomads in Eurasian territory: it ensures the fusion of the Eurasian continent (Chaunu 1977: 62-63); at the same time as the rise of Italian, then European capitalism. This resulted in Europeans bypassing the Muslim Middle East, ultimately leading to the discovery of the Americas by Christopher Columbus and to the beginning of the unification of the world.

In parallel with the diffusions of techniques and sciences from China towards the West, there were cases of diffusion of power techniques or political technology, that is, concrete processes aiming to establish power and control over an area and its population. A political technology consists of structuring an intellectual technology, of a technique in the strict sense of the word and a strategy of control using a power device: this is the case for the postal relays system or for the diverse techniques of taxing populations.

Effectively, technique cannot be separated from politics. For this topic, let us go back to The Muslim Middle East during the premodern period and take a technical example which appears at a glance to be minor. Bulliet stresses the importance of the transition from the saddle known as the south Arabian saddle (mounting a saddle at the back of the dromedary's hump) to the north Arabian saddle (with the saddle on the dromedary's hump) for the Arab-Muslim conquest. The use of this new saddle type, which provided added stability and made the use of other arms possible compared with the south Arabian saddle, gave the Arab-Muslim armies an element of military superiority in mounted combats (Bulliet 1990: 87-110). A military victory often entailed political domination, which thus partially reflects the political effects of a technique. This type of observation does not obviously exclude other political, economic or religious factors. The relationships between nomads and sedentary peoples, the analysis of interior political dynamics in nomadic Arab, Iranian, Turkish or Berber societies (Bonte 1987; Digard 1987) are essential elements which explain certain developments in Muslim civilizations. In the same way as the Baxtyâri Khâns (Digard 1987), the Mongol Ilkhâns from Iran appear to have manipulated the political structure of their society as well as those of nomadic, or even sedentary groups of Iranians, Arabs and Turks in order to establish their power. This playing on political structures and relationships is also present in the Maghreb among Arab and Berber tribes (Bonte 1987). These political "games" had important effects on the constitution and the nature of the technical system, for example on the absence of the road network, as we saw above. Moreover, these interactions and rivalries between nomads and sedentary States had repercussions on the social layer linked to the technical system of these societies, that is, artisans and inventors. The latter – like in China or in Europe – had links with the scholars but they had difficulties in establishing durable links because of the incessant military conflicts between local Muslim powers and the regular nomadic pushes which displaced them. The scholars themselves often had to flee, as they often had ties to such or such Prince, as illustrated by several elements of Ibn Sînâ's biography (Avicenne 1986; Ibn Khaldûn 1980). On the other hand, the very different situation of the literate in ancient China is striking (Métailié 1995). Lastly, if we are to believe the case of the Iranian world, the powers did not always demonstrate a strong interest in technical inventions (Mohebbi 1996). Generally speaking, techniques do not provoke thc same attraction, the same passions as the theoretical sciences such as mathematics or astronomy. In the Middle Ages, in the Muslim world, techniques are accepted by society because they are useful and practical ([13]). However, artisans, technicians and scholars already found it difficult to create continuous, dynamic and effective interaction between them, then with the economic forces and the State, which was the condition leading to industrial development. Authentic engineering schools only began to become established in the Muslim world from the middle of the 19th century onwards (REMMM 1995).

Perhaps what the artisans, technicians and scholars of the Muslim world were lacking is a minimum of *long term stability and security*. With political stability and technical continuity, it would have been possible to create sociotechnical dynamics, leading to the formation of a technical system and an industrial economy. As Weber noted (Weber 1991), these conditions were essential for the establishment of European type capitalism.

The techniques of the Pre-Modern Muslim civilization ([14]) are still poorly studied. Yet, in order to attain expansion and namely architectural realizations, this civilization must have been in possession of specialists and all the technical and scientific knowledge (Al-Hassan et Hill 1991).

In order for new technical development to occur, Man's relationship with nature changes, as does his relationship with the system. In other words, a mechanical image of the world and of systems forms, or a new image, a new perception of nature, bodies and systems. These transformations operated progressively in Europe from the Middle Ages onwards, then the movement continued during the 16th century during which numerous mechanical treatises appeared along with curiosity cabinets, which are one of the symptoms of a new perception of the world (Bredekamp 1996). Then this tendency was definitively confirmed during the 17th and 18th centuries. These conditions do not appear to have been met, *together and in the long term*, in the Pre-Modern Muslim world.

Therefore, much remains to be accomplished in the domain of anthropology and the history of techniques in the Muslim civilization. We dispose of several dispersed studies, which although useful, are often merely descriptions of instruments, tools or machines (Wiet 1996 [1962]; al-Hassan and Hill 1991; Hill 1997; Mohebbi 1996) and do not attempt to assess the technical system in relation to the rest of the social structure ([15]). The study of techniques and their diffusion in the Muslim civilization is important, not only because this area of research has been neglected, but also because this leads to an understanding of the technical system, its links to the economy; sheds light on the differences between it and the Chinese and European systems and thus contributes to a better understanding of the cultural and political system.

The Muslim civilization is set in the midst of Eurasian routes and pathways, inaccurately called "silk routes", as many other types of merchandise were transported and maritime routes were also used. These diverse commercial routes progressively covered the whole of Eurasia and formed circulation and exchange networks for merchandise, money, techniques and ideas. These networks linked this immense space and progressively diffused technical and cultural models in the societies under consideration.

We have seen that technical diffusions is Eurasia occurred through the domestication of equids (horse and donkey), their hybrid (the mule); camelids (dromedary, camel); through the development of means of transport (wagons and steppe carts) and human migrations – particularly those of nomadic peoples; these migrations being accompanied by armed conflicts. There were thus countless exchanges, diffusions, borrowings, integrations, by very ethnically, culturally and politically different societies (agricultural societies to States, nomadic societies, lineage societies).

With the East and West categories, it is not possible to address this space and these societies, their differences and complexities, these creations, these diffusions and exchanges. Even worse, these epistemologically inadequate categories have found a new and dangerous contemporary political formulation in the ideology of the so-called "clash of civilizations".

This is why it is necessary to adopt an approach taking account of diffusions in reflections on the antique, modern and contemporary Eurasian and particularly Muslim worlds.

## IV. Diffusions of techniques and contemporary subjectivation: The globalization of subjectivities

The anthropological debate surrounding globalization has become topical once again after a long period of oblivion. However, the many diffusions continue to raise problems of methods due to identification difficulties. As Herskovits emphasized quite some time ago: "the greatest difficulty in studying processes of invention and discovery, borrowing or diffusion is that we rarely have the opportunity to observe the introduction of new elements in action in a given culture. But in spite of the obstacles and difficulties with the methods, the problem is one of primordial importance and must be tackled. As change is a constant in all systems." (Herskovits 1967: 184).

There is no doubt that the question of diffusion and borrowing is of primordial importance as these phenomena participate today more than ever in a recomposition of identities, even of human nature; and we can only regret, once again, that the issue was neglected for so long by anthropology. Diffusions have raised so many discussions because they bring to light the fact that the societies considered as the most "evolved" by the authors of the 19th and the beginning of the 20th centuries inherited inventions from "savage" or "barbarian" and non-European societies. It is clear that European civilization did not form by itself only on Greek-Roman foundations, but also after successive and decisive borrowing from other worlds, notably in the domains of science and techniques. Braudel rightly wrote that "to accept the reality of these borrowings is to relinquish the West of traditional historians; genially inventing itself from scratch, progressively embarking alone on the pathways of technical and scientific rationality." (Braudel 1979 II: 497).

The perspective referred to as "diffusionist" – moderate or hyperdiffusionist – questioned *in a certain way* the strict evolutionary vision of the development of these human societies, overthrowing the myth of an autonomous evolution. As well as that, this perspective introduced historical analysis into anthropology. Yet history is, as writes Evans Prichard, what part of modern anthropology is built against (Evans-Pritchard 1974). The "diffusionist" approach shook Europe's own representation of its cultural identity. The construction of this identity and the repression that it entailed cannot be separated from the 19ᵗʰ century (period of the emergence of the State-nation and the formation of nationalism), from colonial expansion where self-representation, the representation of culture and history played a central and constitutive ideological role.

This critique of self-representation is also valid for non-European cultures and civilizations confronted to Europe. Indeed, part of their identities were founded on borrowing and represented a reaction against European expansion, which is another way of building. This explains, on one hand, why these cultures do not easily accept today analyses which show that they also borrowed numerous cultural, technical and scientific elements from other civilizations. The current Euro-American economic and techno-scientific domination ([1]) has only accentuated this rejection of so-called western borrowing and influences. Japan is a specific and fascinating case in that it is the only civilization and industrial power to have borrowed massively during its formation, from the 6ᵗʰ century onwards, a large part of what makes up its culture. We are referring to the *kanji* (Japanese name for Chinese characters), to Buddhism, then in the 19th century to the borrowing of the European technical and industrial system. Yet, in spite of large scale borrowing, Japan irrefutably has a strong cultural identity (this is slowly changing and we can observe behavioural Europeanization) and has no profound conflicts with Europe or the United States ([2]). South Korea seems to be in an analogous situation. The problem is more delicate for China and India where relations with the Euro-American world are more complicated, even conflicting, due to the colonial past in India and concessions in China.

The illusory rejection by civilizations of what they owe to others is disastrous since this closes minds to a rigourous historic and anthropological analysis of their history. It is clear that diffusions raise a number of anthropological and political questions concerning the analysis of societies, cultures and the relationships that they have with themselves and with others.

Since the 20th century, the anthropologist can directly observe and analyze considerable quantities of cases of diffusion, borrowing and agnosia in all societies and regions. It is striking that from the 20th century and during the 21st century, everything diffuses in all directions, in all societies and extremely rapidly. This process of diffusion is fundamentally linked to the considerable development of techniques of transport such as the automobile, aviation, railways and communication and information techniques, of which *Internet* is currently one of the most effective vectors; without forgetting the non-negligible role of television, radio and cinema.

At present, the specific question of the impact of the diffusion of techniques – and technosciences – across the world is more relevant than ever. We can resume this point by considering the two main theses which continue to clash with each other. The first advances the idea of a radical technological determinism (Leslie White 1952), a thesis with which Leroi-Gouhran is sometimes wrongly associated (a little too hastily labelled as determinist). The second thesis is anti-determinist and is namely represented in France by Alain Gras, for whom technique is not synonymous with the autonomy it claims to possess (Gras 2003, 1997, 1993). He considers Leroi-Gourhan as an evolutionist in technology. Against these two theories, we affirm that techniques (from the most simple to the most complicated) formed and still form highly decisive devices in that they quickly had inevitable and considerable pervasive effects on essential aspects of structures of societies. It is difficult to argue that there was not a close link between the technique and the industrialization of Europe and thus an over-determination of the technique on the economy and production systems in general. From prehistory onwards, arms and tools play a determining role in the evolution of human groups (Vialou 1996). The same is true of the role of a certain number of techniques in the major transformations which occurred during the Neolithic, Antiquity and the Middle Ages. Emmanuel Le Roy Ladurie clearly that shows that the blocking of economic development in 14th century Languedoc is largely due to what he calls "the technological impasse" (Le Roy Ladurie 1969: 354). The study of diffusions of purely scientific knowledge is much more complex. Indeed, unlike for techniques, the question of conceptual frameworks or paradigms plays a central role in science, like for example the case of the non-diffusion of Chinese medicine in the medieval Muslim world (Gazagnadou 2001b).

The technoscientific and industrial transformations that occurred in Europe from the 18th century onwards did not take place in the Muslim world, or in China. This problem was raised by Needham: for him the cause of the rapid European economic and scientific growth resides in the type of urban revolution and the formation of social classes in open struggle. But is that sufficient? Other parameters must also be taken into account. In Europe, from the Middle Ages onwards, a certain infatuation for technique began to form (Hall 1982; Daumas 1996); then a little later the famous curiosity cabinets appeared in 16th century Europe with quantities of technical objects, varied instruments and machines. These curiosity cabinets were like a new perception of nature, a new awareness of the developing world among the elite and entailed new relationships to machines and technical objects (Bredekamp 1996: 54-55). In the rural world and the artisanal milieu, if techniques did not always immediately give rise to enthusiasm when they developed, they resulted in increased production and revenues (Le Roy Ladurie 1969: 353), which was not without consequences on the perception of technique.

This new relationship to techniques is gauged in certain 17th century texts of famous authors, namely in Descartes' *Discours de la Méthode*. Although he does not propound a real project of technical domination of the world; Descartes' philosophy expresses something new with his theory of the subject, relation to nature, theory of machines, when he writes "Since they [general notions related to physics] made me see that it is possible to develop very useful knowledge applied to life, and that instead of this speculative philosophy taught in schools, we can find a practice through which, with as distinct a knowledge of the force and actions of fire, water, air, stars, skies and all the other bodies surrounding us, as our knowledge of diverse trades and crafts, we could use them in the same way to suitable ends and thus master and possess nature." (Descartes 1966 (1636): 6th part, 84).

In a certain way, this extract sings praise to craftsmen and indirectly calls on applied sciences to create a specialized body, beyond craftsmen. This body is budding as early as the 15th century in Venice where the State founded in 1474 the right of the inventor to monopolize commercialization in virtue of a contract with the State (Hilaire-Pérez: idem: 313). But the creation of corps of engineers required the State's support, which clearly happened in the 18th century in Europe (Hilaire-Pérez 2000: 169). When all these different factors began to interact, as was progressively the case from the Renaissance onwards, they entailed a qualitative leap, a new technological threshold.

From the 17th century and especially during the 18th century; the beginning of industrialization, techniques, natural sciences, the development of the State and economies oriented European thought in this direction referred to as development and industrial progress (Daumas 1996 vol.3).

The major transformation-mutation faced by the whole of humanity since the 20th century is, in substance, that of the setting up of a vast technoscientific device guiding the economic-industrial system and subjectivation modes. As early as 1944, Malinowski wrote: "At present, diffusion is dominating our phase of evolution. Western civilization, like a steamroller, is crushing the surface of the globe. The study of this cultural change, which affects Africa, Asia, Oceania and the New World, makes up most of historic ethnographic research. Anthropology is aware of this and has grasped the extent of the phenomenon" (Malinowski 1968: 180).

European type capitalism and the progressive diffusion of its technical, industrial and cultural system across the entire planet was anticipated by M. Mauss and G. Tarde over a century ago. For them, this movement was part of technical progress. This notion of technical progress, intrinsically linked to the diffusion of the European industrial technical system, was also to lead to the transfer of technology from the industrialized countries towards developing countries. There is a theoretical link between the study of techniques and their diffusions for pre-modern periods and the transfer of technology for contemporary periods (Cresswell 1983: 143-159). However, if pre-modern diffusions are transfers of techniques carried out – voluntarily or not – by individuals or small literary groups or even by certain powers (for example, the Arab translations of Greek texts), we cannot compare them to the transfers of technologies planned by States or institutions. But in both cases, these are diffusions of techniques and knowledge according to specific modalities. Only the scale, the organization and the effects vary. The upheavals of technical systems are clearly much more widespread and problematic today; in this respect, it is necessary to resume the 1970s debate on the transfer of technology and questions of development. These transfers of technology raise more problems than solutions as far as the transfers of large industrial units are concerned. The critical debates conducted by anthropologists, sociologists and economists on development *sometimes* allow certain types of transfers of techniques and technical knowledge to be carried out in good conditions for Third World countries. However, given the failings of these transfers of technology, during the 1970s there was a development of what was to be called appropriate technologies, mixing modern technologies and local intelligence ($^3$). But it soon became clear that these appropriate technologies could not resolve the industrial problems raised by economic development, particularly in the context of globalization. The huge gap between the new technical system (and its interlocking with sciences) and the technical systems of Third World countries was and still is a major problem.

These transfers also raise serious cultural problems. Indeed, it was soon proved that techniques cannot be transferred without taking account of the technocultural system of the country or the region involved. We just have to recall the incredible blunders committed in the different Third World countries, like the case of the industrialization of Algeria or in the domain of agriculture, with the setting up of socialist agricultural villages: two cases of poorly thought out transfers which led to human and economic catastrophes (Bairoch 1992, Gras 1993: 261-267). The brutal imposition of industrial activities on a traditional agrarian society could only lead to the production of poor quality objects and tools, as a long experience and long training periods are required to ensure success in this domain. It also entails the dissolution of traditional familial or village solidarity, forcing these populations into economic and identity disarray.

The incredible development of techniques and science in the 20th century and notably the development and increasing speed of transport and communication began to radically and irrevocably change our world. This technoscientific development is linked to that of energy awareness as Mumford shows, with a slightly rigid breakdown into major technical phases: eotechnical (water-wood complex), paleotechnical (coal-iron complex) and neotechnical (electricity–alloys) (Mumford 1950: 105-107) and to the setting up of technical macro systems such as the railway or electricity (Gras 1993: 17-18 and chap. 5). These spectacular technoscientific and industrial developments led to new sociological and political analyses from the beginning of the 20th century onwards, especially in the Frankfurt School. This trend of thought understood that sciences and techniques had become a central part of the development of industrial societies which modified the conditions of production in capitalism, systems of perception and the cultural and affective behaviour of individuals (Marcuse 1968; Horkheimer & Adorno 1974; Habermas 1973, see also Friedmann 1966, who has no link with the Frankfurt School). This led Habermas to emit the hypothesis that science and technique had become, not just the new ideology of the European, or even worldwide cultural system, but that they were the main productive forces in contemporary economies (Habermas 1973: 36).

Did this movement adhere to the first technical skill, caught up itself in a biological dynamic, as Leroi-Gouhran thought? It was certainly part of it but perhaps not as radically, irreversibly and systematically as he thought. Let us just acknowledge that technical determinism exists to a certain extent: from the hoe to the plough, from the plough to the cart, there is a technical logic (Mazoyer 1997; Haudricourt 1986) in the internal development of these instruments and because, as Leroi-Gouhran writes "one does not exchange a cart for a plough or a hoe". Cases of technical regression, envisaged by Leroi-Gouhran, are relatively rare and often linked to major natural catastrophes or wars. Everywhere in the world, technical tendencies are updated as techniques increase practically all forms of production and allow for new creations, on an individual or group scale. They are either materialized, as we saw, directly by simultaneous invention, or else later by diffusion.

Technical (and therefore cultural) diffusions have affected the whole of the globe exponentially throughout the centuries, in a movement of immense proliferation where it is difficult to identify the limits. Given these processes, Leroi-Gourhan and Lévi-Strauss always maintained a clear demarcation line between *technical evolution* and *ethical evolution* (Leroi-Gourhan 1943 & 1945; Lévi-Strauss 1961); since, to put it mildly, technical and scientific progress and economic development are not, in many cases, in keeping with any sort of ethical stance.

Beyond the ethical issue, diffusion on a worldwide scale remains a complex question for anthropology, whatever the resistance, and introduces a new and similar way of being and perception, especially among young people. These contemporary diffusions are characterized by multiple and massive borrowing in very varied cultural domains and seem to be accompanied by the diffusion of European individualism.

Let us take several small examples: the history of Levis jeans is emblematic in this respect. A Bavarian peddler called Levi-Strauss arrived in California in 1853 intending to sell tent canvas. He realized that there was more demand for trousers than tents and set up the production of solid trousers, which were put on the market in 1860. Thus began the major worldwide diffusion of Levis (Boulay 1999: 45).

The example of the washing machine is another case of worldwide diffusion (Delaunay 1999). This technical object was invented in the United-States at the beginning of the 20th century, spread almost throughout the entire world and considerably changed the situation of women.

In the domain of music, the case of rock and derived music is just as remarkable. Meeting young people in the Teheran mountains gathered around a tape recorder listening to a *Cheb Khaled* song, a star of *raï* music and translated into Persian in New York, is not only a surprising experience, but also backs up our hypotheses. Indeed, if we take these three tiny cases, it becomes clear that they contributed to major subjective and socio-cultural transformations: jeans and the washing machine affected women's place in society (women were not allowed to wear trousers for a long time): rock and its by-products changed relations between men and women throughout the world. In the domain of sport, the case of football in Iran raises the question of the reasons for the worldwide diffusion not just of a sport but also of a type of subjective individualist attitude (Bromberger 1998). One of the consequences of this in Iran is the decline of the traditional Iranian struggle, the *zurkhâne* (Rochard 2000).

The television is a better known case. The influence of television programs transmitted by satellite and more or less legally received, on the ideas and behaviour of certain populations is very perceptible. In Iran, we have noticed contradictory, complex and variable reactions to Euro-American, Turkish or Japanese programs depending on the social layer: a mixture of attraction and rejection of the programs where relations between men and women are too direct. On the other hand, the success of the Japanese series *Oshin*, diffused on national television, exhibited more connivance between certain aspects of Iranian and Japanese cultures (modesty in relations between men and women, strong familial solidarity, respect for the elders, etc.). Another interesting case is that of plastic surgery. More and more Iranians, including men, are having recourse to plastic surgery, particularly for the nose. They consider that their noses are too big and adopt small European or American style noses as their model. This is their experience, whether or not this is true is a different matter. This trend began to spread in the 1950s in ruling circles and then diffused through society, especially when surgical techniques improved and made it possible to have several operations at an affordable price (Gazagnadou 2006). The same kind of influence is visible in Japan where more than 20,000 women have their eyes surgically opened each year, in order to have "big eyes" like European or American women. All these cultural influences which affect these countries because of new transport and communication techniques are – in vain – opposed by Iranian and Chinese powers. These powers try to curb the diffusion of behaviour with ideas contrary to traditions. Once again, it is important to underline the close relationship between technique and politics.

The question of relationships between cultures and subjectivities has been radically changed and amplified by the fact that technical means of communication (radio, television, post, Internet) and transport (bicycle, motorcycle, automobile, boat and plane) developed in extraordinary proportions. These techniques, machines and technical objects were diffused on a worldwide scale and, unlike what happened during pre-modern periods, other techniques were diffused by these means entailing subjective and mental transformations among wider human groups, thereby transforming traditional frameworks and societies' visions of the world. At the heart of these upheavals, sexuality, individual pleasures and leisure played a central role. Technical devices played a determining role in all these cases, as they generally do.

These examples bring us back to a major question, which is more important than ever in anthropology: a new subjectivation mode developed everywhere, as it was called following Foucault. This mode stems partly from antique Greece, and partly from Christianity which reorganized certain aspects of Greek thought by introducing the idea of equality for all (before God) in a logic of salvation; which is very different from the Greek individual and collective agonistic behaviour. This subjectivation mode is a type of relationship to the self based on a relationship to others, which incites the individual to think and live like a subject, autonomous and free from all determinism. Greek invention in politics is linked to the emergence of this subjectivation: separating the relationship to the self from the relationship with others, folding power into itself, to put it into relation to others as generalized rivalry (Deleuze 1986). This completely new subjectivation mode has familiar consequences on the conception, political practice and functioning of the Greek City (evidently for the free citizen as equality is not Greek): rhetorical rivalry with whomever (political isonomy); collective deliberation; possibility to challenge all elected representatives (Finley 1985), etc. This is an invention of a radically new politically practice that no society had ever known. Then although Christianized, European culture perpetuated this relationship to politics in its city towns, as a form of resistance against feudal, royal and papal powers until the French Revolution and the present.

This new, strange and problematic subjectivation mode for the older generations of traditional societies, is (and was) materially backed up by the development of techniques and the diffusion across the globe of the same worldwide industrial techno-economic system. For the most part, this would have affected the Eurasian axis between 10,000 years before the Christian era and the 20th century.

From the 20th century onwards, the "Greek-European" subjectivation mode (as far as the political figure and the individual subject are concerned) diffused throughout the world, was borrowed and, as Tarde would say, imitated. This is particularly manifest in the worldwide desire of representative and direct political representation, equality, rights for all, children's' rights, male-female parity, etc. This is the movement which we refer to as the euro-hellenisation of the world, or let us say a certain euro-hellenisation. Deep-rooted movements shake up all populations and all societies as, through communication techniques, they become aware of the ongoing changes throughout the world. They also participate in a complex and contradictory manner in this new global subjective paradigm. This worldwide subjective movement is so striking that we are tempted to speak of the "subjective tendency of the individual-subject", just as Leroi-Gouhran spoke of technical tendency. All this happens as if we were witnessing the materialization of subjective virtualities, either directly or by diffusion, as soon as the context makes it possible. This subjective tendency is linked and joined to the technical tendency. If we take the case of the post, we can clearly see that the technical tendency (the technical postal device) and the subjective tendency (writing and becoming the subject) materialized everywhere but were staggered throughout time depending on the societies and cultures. Effectively, from the time that postal services outside Europe began to transport individual correspondence, the same subjective effects of individualization became apparent in very different cultural areas. The history of the car is an example of the materialization of the technical tendency of self-displacement which is designed around individual history, first in Europe, then across the globe, with familiar effects: ease of movement, exchanges, individual and collective meetings, but also unfortunately pollution, destruction of certain natural environments...

It is ideologies of national-cultural identity as well as narrow evolutionism which conditioned many anthropological approaches, preventing us from addressing the evolution of Man and societies in this new anthropological-historic perspective combining the technoeconomic system, diffusion, subjective arrangement, new transformations, etc., in an endless historic process. It is an evolution in the sense of growth, through the technique, effectiveness on environments and an expansion of the territories of individual and societal creativity. Just like the way writing, the new intellectual technology representing invention and diffusion, broadened individual boundaries (Goody 1979: 86-87).

The diffusion on a global scale of the same technoeconomic system, or new globalization phase as it is a process which has never ceased, radically transformed the subjectivation modes of all societies. We referred to this above as the Euro-hellenisation of the world, not to reproduce the old idea of the Greek miracle, nor to overvalue a culture in relation to others, but to underline what is observed everywhere, namely the emergence of the individual-subject. This way of being, this relation to the self which wants to break away from traditions, from the rules of society in which and for which the referent must remain what is done "because that was what was done". If these societies (Japan, China, India but also in Africa and South Asia) retain strong identities, case studies show that the same subjectivation mode is developing there among the youth and certain social layers as in Europe. We thus see members of societies of non-Euro-American culture, especially the young people, taking their own desires, their own wishes as their only reference, however illusory that may be. They want to enjoy life as they please, to choose their studies themselves, to marry who they choose, divorce or separate according to their own criteria and not those of the extended family; to travel; on a political level, to give themselves the right to participate, to choose their party, their movement, to speak and write when they wish; in sum, to construct their own individual-subject in relation to a self-referential me ([4]). Yet, these so-called modern modalities (even though we do not clearly understand what being modern means) are the product of certain aspects of antique Greek culture, revamped during the course of European history, in the domains of politics and individuation.

We fundamentally agree with the theses of Arjun Appadurai who clearly recognizes that the emergence and the development of communication techniques, in the broad sense of the term, form the basis for changes which allow individuals to envisage new possibilities in life in very different parts of the planet. Appadurai writes: "a transformation has taken place these past decades, a change based on technological innovations which occurred about a century ago..." (Appadurai 2001: 30). This idea was already present in the work on Mauss and Leroi-Gourhan; just like other concepts – which are sometimes used in debatable ways – come from the writings of Deleuze and Guattari (1972 and 1980). The notion of imagination used by Appadurai is somewhat simplistic compared to those of deterritorialization, which refer to a conception of desire as a machine of permanent new combinations. Transport and communication techniques were fundamental but they do not fully explain this global diffusion and the rupture of individuals with the traditions of their societies. What added dynamics therefore made them possible? It is the arrangement of techniques, science, capitalism and a subjectivation mode which produced an individual-subject. This arrangement took place in Europe and formed a hybrid arrangement in constant recombination. In this immense rhizomatic machine, the modalities of expression and desire of the individual-subject are hugely increased, for better and for worse. And the arrangement with technologies and the speed of diffusion play a fundamental role in this process. The speed with which new behaviours form and the creation of new means are subjective factors in the deterritorialization and disintegration of the usual cultural contexts. Many technique thinkers panic when confronted with the deployment of the technoscientific system, as Gabor's law is always lurking in the background ("what can happen will happen" or "everything possible will be done necessarily"). This anguish stems from the fact that they still consider the subject as defined in Europe since Antiquity, that is to say, separated from nature, from his technical milieu, from politics and from desire. At each historical period in each society, techniques and their diffusion entailed the formation of new layouts which could be both enslaving and simultaneously inventive for the group and for individuals.

# V. Epilogue

During the 19th century, anthropologists referred to as diffusionists opened up paths for understanding the transformations of societies. Today, it is important to study technical, technoscientific diffusions and the ensuing subjective and cultural transformations in greater depth. But at the same time, in this vast diffusion movement, it is relevant to question pseudo progress, such as the sorry spectacle currently provided in almost every country by certain televisual and "cultural" programs ([1]).

The diffusion of a new technical system, of ever more effective machines and instruments which transform our subjective universes (Sakhara 2004), our sensitivities, our perceptions ([2]) and our behaviour, is irreversible. These transformations are visible in very different terrains such as Japan, Iran, Egypt, Morocco and Europe. Diffusion anthropology requires a careful and micro-political ethnography, based on small events, concrete facts and minor behavioural modifications. Through the analysis of concrete diffusion cases it is crucial to grasp the major re-compositions of affective and subjective universes in which individuals and all societies are engaged. A major transformation has begun and new subjective humans-techniques-sciences layouts are forming, accompanied by a re-composition of our cognitive universes.

Contemporary anthropology must thus re-examine, continue and further the study of the diffusions of techniques. These latter are increasingly numerous and faster with ever more powerful transforming effects. Paul Virilio showed the political nature of this from the point of view of the relations between the speed factor and contemporary perception (Virilio 1977 & 1993). Moreover, the speed to which Virilio refers is closely related to the speed at which human beings and information travel.

As early as 1944, Malinowski, a self-proclaimed adversary of *diffusionism*, nonetheless underlined the importance and the radically new character of diffusions in the 20th century. For Claude Lévi-Strauss, this diffusion of European civilization on a global scale raises serious issues concerning the identity, the diversity and the standardization or even the disappearance of cultures (Lévi-Strauss 1961). The observation and the study of diffusions of all types raise the question of the radical transformation of cultures oriented towards increasingly shared thought based on techniques and sciences. A new layout of technosciences, minds and cultures is currently being formed and is an integral part of the new subjectivation mode. This is a new global way for individuals to organize their relationships with themselves, with others and with the world. Unfortunately, in our opinion, this does not mean that this process occurs without contradictions, conflicts and suffering.

This set of questions related to contacts and diffusions between civilizations, to cultural identities, to the future of cultures, which Levi-Strauss saw in the middle of the last century as being "ahead of us" (Lévi-Strauss 1961), is *already among us*. At this stage of the 21st century, anthropology is confronted with this, as are all the peoples who are currently living and will live through these phenomena.

It is to be hoped that anthropology will fully apply what A. N. Whitehead wrote of the purpose of reason, namely, "to encourage the art of living" (Whitehead 1969: 105). Of course, diffusion anthropology will not do this alone, it is neither its aim, nor within its capacity; and any will to create a system makes no sense today and would probably only raise a number of problems. Other modes of thinking must be associated with anthropology since, as Kroeber wrote 'There is no correct way and bad way for making anthropology progress: we need them all (Krieger 1961); "temperate diffusionism", neodiffusionism or symmetrical anthropology.

In the face of the massive and rapid diffusions of the contemporary and globalized world, diffusion anthropology can contribute, especially through the analysis of the diffusions of techniques, to understanding the transformations to come and encourage the art of living and the –

controlled – opening of cultures to each other. This does not mean the whole identity of all societies. However, this global orientation is in the process of transforming the human being. The individual is involved in vast networks and simultaneously metamorphoses into a new type of individual, who can be controlled remotely by power devices but who is also inevitably capable of producing new forms of resistance. A new arrangement of the human and of technoscience is currently forming with results which remain unpredictable and unthinkable.

In this new historic phase, we cannot see why this new individual and these new social productions would not produce, once again, differences of subjective creations, except if we forget that "difference resides in repetition" (Deleuze, 1968: 103).

This new historic phase in just a new historical layout but cannot solely be reasoned with concepts issued from ancient critiques of techniques and sciences. All the more so since anthropology must now deal with a new question linked to the global diffusion of the same techno-industrial system: that of ecology. Indeed, the industrial economy seriously degrades and threatens all the life forms of the planet.

Through the technique, industrialization then technoscience, the human being wished to and succeeded in controlling individuals and societies but destroyed many natural environments, societies and individuals in the process. Today, all life forms are at stake. A logic of destruction has been added to the biopower and the surveillance brought to light by Foucault.

This situation calls for new political, technical, scientific and economic responses. This ecological devastation may compel the techno-economic system to a new re-adaptation. The threats weighing on our ecosystem and on all life forms must lead to a change in the relations between economy, technology and way of life. This situation is unprecedented in human history, radically new for natural environments and for Man himself. It calls into question, for the first time, the anthropisation of the world. The creation of new ways of thinking thus becomes an ethical and political demand, particularly as far as techniques, technosciences and their rapid diffusion into societies are concerned. The anthropology of technical and cultural diffusions wishes to contribute to these necessary reorientations.

# NOTES

INTRODUCTION

1. Otherwise stated, this viewpoint is well summarized and defended by Jean-Pierre Warnier: "On one hand, they [the ethnologists] attest a rapid and irreversible erosion of singular cultures on a planetary scale. On the other, in practice [...] they observe that this erosion is limited by concrete elements of cultures-traditions and that there is a constant abundant and diversified cultural production throughout the world, in spite of the cultural hegemony exerted by industrialized countries" (Warnier 1999: 78)

2. We will not employ the concept of acculturation; J. F. Baré demonstrated the shortcomings of the term (Baré 1991).

3. The Maghreb is "integrated" into Eurasia here, as it inherits traits from Middle East civilizations, particularly through Islamic expansion.

4. Average dates for the main domestications of plants and cereals, animals and for the main inventions in Eurasia: plants and cereals between 15,000 and 7,000 B.C. (Guilaine 2000); dog: around 15,000 B.C.; horse, camel, dromedary, buffalo: around 3,000 B.C. (Vigne 2004, Digard 1990); beginning of agriculture between 12,500 and 9,000 B.C. (Guilaine 2000, Cauvin 1997), metallurgy (3,000-4,000 B.C.); wheeled vehicles 3,000 B.C. (Littauer & Crouwel 1979); writing 3,300 B.C. (Herrenschmidt 2007); gunpowder 1,044 A.D. (Needham 1973); paper: 1st century A.D. (Carter 1925).

5. All animal species are not "domesticable": among equids, for example, the fact that the zebra does not appear to be domesticable (apart from very brief and late domestication experiments) was not without techno-economic, political and military consequences for African societies (Swart 2003; I wish to thank J. Olivier Le Gall for kindly communicating references concerning the zebra). The consequences of horse and camelid domestication for Eurasian societies require no commentary. The non-domestication of certain animals has very different origins: for example, according to Descola, the Indians never domesticated the tapir because they believed that they had a particular link to the animal world, making the tapir a relative, and relatives are not to be subjugated (Descola: 1994: 329-344). For further reading on domestication and non-domestication see Digard 1990.

6. Recently Diamond advanced certain interesting arguments concerning the influence of the environment of the history of societies but his very environmentalist approach totally neglects political aspects (Diamond 2000).

Chapter I

1. We find very partial and biased diffusionist theses from the 19th century and the first half of the 20th century, in among others: Löwie, *Histoire de l'ethnologie classique*, 1937, French trans., 1971, Payot Editions, Paris; in Mercier, *Histoire de l'anthropologie*, PUF Editions, Paris, 1966; see also Descola, Lenclud, Severi, Taylor, *Les idées de l'anthropologie*, A. Colin Editions, Paris, 1988; Poirier, "Histoire de la pensée ethnologique" in *Ethnologie Générale*, Gallimard Editions, La Pléiade, Paris, 1968; Rupp-Eisenreich, "Diffusionnisme" 1991; Stocking, *After Tylor, British Social Anthropology 1888-1951*, Athlone, London, 1996.

2. Construction of stone monuments for solar cults.

3. The censor of diffusionist writings continued for quite some time. This was the case for the review *The new diffusionist* published in England between 1971 and 1974 which was refused for publication in *Antiquity*, its theoretical positions being qualified as "nonsense". Cf. *New diffusionist*, 5, October 1971.

4. It is important to emphasize the long-term notion as everyone knows that the Indians won some battles against white men.

5. See Tocqueville's short text, *Quinze jours dans le désert américain*, in which the author describes the ravages produced by alcohol among Indian populations during his journey in America in the middle of the 19th century (Tocqueville 1998 [1860]).

6. "...Firstly, we must declare that our research has not in any way divulged the preponderant influence that Mr. Tarde attributes to imitation in the genesis of collective facts. [...] Moreover, we can ask ourselves if imitation is a suitable word for designating propagation due to coercive influence. This single expression confuses very different phenomena which require differentiation." (Durkheim 1937: note 1, p. 12, see also the preface to the second edition p. XVII).

7. We know that G. Montandon was a member of the Commission for Jewish affairs of the Vichy government and that he made a "political science" out of his ethnology, for the distinction of races. This is paradoxical as he affirms that diffusion and borrowing determine the construction of cultures and yet, at the same time, he collaborates in the destruction of Jews in Europe, because of the potential danger of Jews mixing with Europeans!

Chapter II

1. "It is up to us, the successors, to ask why we have left technology to stagnate for so long" (Creswell 1996: 330).

2 In particular in the review *Techniques et Culture*.

3. It should be clear that if we include language in means of communication, it is not reduced to this sole aspect, cf. for example, Benveniste 1966: chap V.

4. In the Maghreb, the transport question is the same as in the Middle East. The first "roads" date from the Roman period; with the end of Roman domination, transport was carried out by pack animals; wheeled vehicles were introduced through colonization

from the 19ᵗʰ century onwards.

5. Like the two-wheeled trolley (Gazagnadou 2007).

6. In the case of Indonesia, see the scandal brought on by the concerts of the singer/ dancer *Inul Daratista* during her pop music concerts (*Inul, la chanteuse qui ensorcelle l'Indonésie, Le Nouvel Observateur*, n° 2024, 21-27 August 2003). In the same way Iranian powers are opposed to all rock or pop concerts.

CHAPTER III

1. We did not mention Japan here as, curiously, since the 20ᵗʰ century, this country is no longer included in the Eastern category, or when it is, it is only from an esthetic, artistic or traditional daily life viewpoint.

2. In Europe, as A. Grosrichard has shown, the notion of Asian despotism was widely used, especially in the 18ᵗʰ century to show —and to oppose- the problem of absolute power and the limits which should be imposed on the State (Grosrichard 1979: chap. II).

3. On this question see Marx's texts published in: "Sur les sociétés précapitalistes", *Centre d'Etudes et de Recherches Marxistes (C.E.R.M)*, Editions Sociales, Paris, 1978. For debates between Marxists, see also "Sur le mode production asiatique", *Centre d'Etudes et de Recherches Marxistes (C.E.R.M)*, Editions sociales, Paris, 1974. Among Marx's writings, see namely: "Formes précapitalistes de la production, types de proprié-té" in *Principes d'une critique de l'économie politique (1857-1858), Œuvres, Economie II*, Editions Gallimard, coll. La Pléiade, 1968. Marx "Réponse à Mikhailovski (November 1877)", "Réponse de Marx à Vera Zassoulitch" (8 March 1881), p. 1557-1558, and "Brouillons de la réponse de Marx à Vera Zassoulitch", p. 1559-1573, in *Œuvres, Economie II*, Editions Gallimard, coll. La Pléiade, 1968; and Marx's letter to Engels from June 2ⁿᵈ 1853 in *"Lettres sur Le Capital"*, Editions Sociales, Paris, 1964, p. 61.

4. « [...] Bernier rightly discerns the fundamental form of all phenomena from the East – he speaks of Turkey, of Persia and Hindustan – in that there is no private property ownership. And that is the veritable key, even of the eastern sky... » (Marx 1964: 61).

5. The caste system is visible on a socio-economic level in the *jajmani* system: a system of benefits based on castes and professions: certain Brahman castes are constrained to use certain casts of launderers who themselves must employ a certain subcaste of Muslim dancers (Dumont 1966).

6. Hegel read widely on all Chinese, Brahman, Iranian and other religions (Hegel 1990 I: 234-247 and 1990 II: 62-155).

7. This disagreement with Goody does not call into question the interest and the beauty of his analyses.

9. Although the Muslim world was a civilization of borrowing and diffusions, that does not mean that we believe that the Muslim world only played a transmitting role, which underplays its role as a creator.

10. We are interested in the general aspect, we have no competence in the domain of mathematics.

11. Roshdi Rashed writes: "Three years later, the mathematician and Arabist Golius,

returning to the Near East with a crop of mathematical manuscripts – including a copy of "Algebra" by al-Khayyâm – submitted the Pappus problem to Descartes, which was to profoundly affect his mathematical thought" (Rashed 1999: 17). Was Descartes aware of the contents of Khayyâm's text? For R. Rashed the question remains unanswered. We understand R. Rashed's scientific caution, but on the basis of his writings it is nonetheless difficult not to opt for the hypothesis of a decisive diffusion from the Muslim world towards Europe.

12. This is the invocation: "In the name of Allah, The Clement, The Merciful", which must precede all writing, according to the Muslim tradition.

13. Like in Europe.

14. The Arab language employs the term *hiyal* to designate techniques: an ingenious mechanism.

15. The book by P. Mohebbi (1996) is one of the rare attempts at trying to understand the non-development of a technical industrial system in the Iranian part of the pre-Modern Muslim civilization. Our disagreement with this author mainly concerns the over-systematic use of the concept of *mentality*, which leads him, for example, to explain the absence of wheeled vehicles in Iran by the existence of a *mentality without wheels*. This is too abstract an analysis, a little short, which ignores technical and political aspects.

CHAPTER IV

1. Domination to which we must add Japan, Russia and soon China, India and Brazil. In many countries, Japan is often forgotten even though it participates actively in this domination.

2. With the United States, the resentment concerns the atomic bombarding of Hiroshima and Nagasaki and the presence of American bases in Okinawa.

3. See a case of appropriate technology in a hospital in Teheran concerning the adaptation of a hairdresser's chair into a computer destined to diagnose vertigo (Gazagnadou 1999 b).

4. This is where we diverge from J.-P. Warnier's analysis, as he sees globalization as an erosion of local cultures but also as a recomposition of local cultures, which he calls the machine which produces the difference.

CHAPTER V

1. In order to gauge the "originality" and the "quality" of these programs, it suffices to look at several programs (by satellite or cable) on Chinese, Korean, Arab, Iranian and European stations. The reader will immediately understand what we mean by sorry spectacle.

2. G. Friedmann observed this in a stimulating collection of case studies (Friedmann 1966).

# BIBLIOGRAPHY

JOURNALS

ANNALES, Histoire, Sciences Sociales, Histoire des techniques, 1998, n°4-5, Juillet-Octobre. Editions de l'EHESS. Paris.

Revue du Monde Musulman et de la Méditerranée (REMMM), n°72, 1995 : « Modernités arabes et turques : maîtres et ingénieurs ». Editions Edisud, Aix-en-Provence.

BOOKS AND ARTICLES

ADORNO Theodor. W. & HORKHEIMER Max
1974 *La dialectique de la raison*, [1961], Editions Gallimard, coll. Tel, Paris.

ABDEL-MALEK Anouar
1969, *Idéologie et renaissance nationale. L'Egypte moderne*, 2ème édition, Editions Anthropos, Paris.

Al-HASSAN Ahmad. Y. et HILL Donald. R.
1991 *Sciences et techniques en Islam*, Editions Edifra & Unesco, Paris.

AMBROSE Stanley H.
2001 « Paleolithic Technology and Human Evolution » *Science*, March, vol. 291, pp. 1748-1753.

ANDERSON Perry
1978 *L'Etat Absolutiste II*, Editions François Maspero, Paris.

APPADURAI, Arjun
2001 *Après le colonialisme, les conséquences culturelles de la globalisation*, Editions Payot, Paris.

ARISTOTE
1993 *Les Politiques*, (traduction inédite, introduction, bibliographie, notes et index par Pierre Pellegrin), 2eme édition revue et corrigée, Editions GF. Flammarion, Paris.

AVICENNE
1986 *Le livre de science*, Editions Les Belles Lettres & Unesco, Paris.

AYALON David
1996 *La phénomène mamelouk dans l'Orient islamique*, Editions des PUF, Paris.

BALANDIER Georges
1984 *Anthropologie Politique*(1968), Editions des PUF, coll. Quadrige, Paris.

BALFET Hélène
1975 «Technologie», in Robert Cresswell, *Eléments d'ethnologie 2*, Editions A. Colin, Paris.

BARE Jean-François
1991 « Acculturation » in *Dictionnaire de l'ethnologie et de l'anthropologie* (sous la direction de P. Bonte et M. Izard), PUF, Paris.

BASALLA George
1988 *The evolution of technology*, Cambridge University Press, Cambridge.

BASTIAN Adolf
1887 «Notices sur les pierres sculptées du Guatemala, récemment acquises par le Musée Royal d'Ethnographie de Berlin», in *Annales du Musée Guimet*, tome 10, 1887, p. 264-305, Editeur E. Leroux, Paris.

BATESON Grégory
1971 *La cérémonie du Naven*, Editions de Minuit/ Livre de poche, Biblio/Essais, Paris.
1977 *Vers une écologie de l'esprit 1*, Editions du Seuil, Paris.
1996 *Une unité sacrée, quelques pas de plus vers une écologie de l'esprit*, Editions du Seuil, Paris.

BAUSINGER Hermann
1993 *Volkskunde ou l'ethnologie allemande*, Editions de la Maison des sciences de l'homme, Paris.

BECQUEMONT Daniel
1992 *Darwin, darwinisme, évolution*, Editions Kimé, Paris.

BENVENISTE Emile
1966 *Problèmes de linguistique générale*, Editions Gallimard, col. Tel. vol.1, Paris.

BERGSON Henri
1941 *L'évolution créatrice* (1907), Editions des PUF, coll. Quadrige, Paris.

BERNIER François
1981 *Voyage dans les Etats du Grand Mogol* [1670-1671], Editions Fayard, Paris.

BLOCH Marc
1983a «Les transformations des techniques comme problème de psychologie collective» (1948) in *Mélanges Historiques* Tome II, Serge Fleury éditeur, Editions de l'EHESS, Paris,
1983b «Avènement et conquête du moulin à eau (1935) in *Mélanges Historiques*, Tome II.
1983c «Les "inventions" médiévales» (1935) in *Mélanges Historiques*, Tome II.
1983d «Technique et évolution sociale : réflexions d'un historien» [1938] in *Mélanges Historiques*, Tome II.

BOAS Franz
1924 "Evolution or diffusion", in *Race,language and culture*(1940) p.290-294, University of Chicago Press, Chicago and London.
1932 *Anthropology and modern life*, Dover Publications Inc., New York.

BONNAUD Robert
1989 *Le système de l'Histoire*, Editions Fayard, Paris.

BONTE Pierre
1987 «Les Awlad Qaylan, donneurs de femmes ou preneurs d'hommes?», *L'Homme,* n°102, XXVII (2), Paris.
1992 «Après Leroi-Gourhan : tendances et problèmes d'une approche ethnologique des faits techniques», in *Les nouvelles de l'archéologie*, 48/49, (été-automne), Paris.

1999 «Travail, techniques et valeur, contributions (nouvelles) au débat sur rites et techniques», in *Dans le sillage des techniques. Hommage à Robert Cresswell*, Editions L'Harmattan, Paris.

BONTE Pierre et IZARD Michel (sous la direction)
1991 *Dictionnaire de l'Ethnologie et de l'Anthropologie*, 2ème édition, Editions des PUF, Paris.

BOULAY Anne
1999 -«Les objets du siècle : le jean», in *Libération*, 19 septembre, p.44-45.

BRAUDEL Fernand
1979 *Civilisation matérielle, Economie et capitalisme. XVe-XVIIIe siècle*
T.1 : Les structures du quotidien.
T.2 : Les jeux de l'échange.
T.3 : Le temps du monde.
1969 *Ecrits sur l'Histoire*, Editions Flammarion, coll. Champs, Paris.

BRIANT Pierre
1982 *Etat et pasteurs au Moyen-Orient ancien*, Cambridge University Press et Editions de la Maison des Sciences de l'Homme, Paris.

BROMBERGER Christian
1998 *Football, la bagatelle la plus sérieuse du monde*, Editions Bayard, Paris.
1997 «L'ethnographie de la France par les romanistes de l'école de Hambourg», in *Mots et choses de l'ethnographie de la France (Regards allemands et autrichiens sur la France rurale dans les années 30)*, K. Beilt, Ch. Bromberger, I. Chiva (éditeurs), Editions de la Maison des Sciences de l'Homme, Paris.
1990 -«Un demi-siècle après : redécouvrir les travaux de l'école romaniste de Hambourg», in W. Giese, *Mots et choses en Haut-Dauphiné dans les années 30*, Le monde alpin et rhodanien, 3/4.

CAHEN Claude
1995 *L'islam, des origines au début de l'empire ottoman*, Editions Bordas, Paris.
1962 «Les facteurs économiques et sociaux dans l'ankylose culturelle

de l'Islam», in *Classicisme et déclin culturel dans l'histoire de l'Islam*, Editions G. P. Maisonneuve et Larose, Paris.

CALMARD Jean
1987 « Les marchands iraniens (Formation et montée d'un groupe de pression, 16ᵉ-19ᵉ siècles) » in *Marchands et hommes d'affaires asiatiques*, Editions de l'EHESS, Paris.

CANGUILHEM Georges
1985 *La connaissance de la vie*, Editions J. Vrin, Paris
1962 *Du développement à l'évolution au XIXe siècle*, Editions des PUF (coll. Pratiques théoriques), Paris.

CARTER Thomas Francis
1925 *The invention of printing in China and its spread westward*, Columbia University Press, New York.

CAUVIN Jacques
1994 *Naissance des divinités, Naissance de l'Agriculture*, Editions du CNRS, Paris.

CENTRE D'ETUDES ET DE RECHERCHES MARXISTES (C.E.R.M)
1974 «Sur "le mode de production asiatique"», Editions Sociales, Paris.
1978 «Sur les sociétés précapitalistes», Editions Sociales, Paris.

CHAUNU Pierre
1977 « Les mondes en miettes » in *L'ouverture du monde, XIVe-XVe siècles, Histoire économique et sociale du monde, tome 1*, Editions Armand Colin, Paris.

CHILDE Gordon
1964 *La naissance de la civilisation*, Editions Gonthier, bibliothèque Médiations, Paris.
1961 *De la Préhistoire à l'Histoire*, Editions Gallimard, coll. Idées, Paris.

CHIVA Isac & JEGGLE Utz (Essais réunis par)
1987 *Ethnologies en miroir. La France et les pays de langue allemande*, Editions de la Maison des sciences de l'homme, Paris.

CRESSWELL Robert
1996 *Prométhée ou Pandore ? Propos de technologie culturelle*, Editions Kimé, Paris
1975 *Eléments d'Ethnologie 1. Huit terrains*, Editions A. Colin, Paris.
*Eléments d'Ethnologie 2. Six approches*, Editions A. Colin, Paris.
1994 «La nature cyclique des relations entre la technique et le social. Approche technologique de la chaîne opératoire», in B. Latour & P. Lemonnier, *De la préhistoire aux missiles balistiques*.
1983 «Transferts de techniques et chaînes opératoires», in *Techniques et culture*, n° 2, Juillet-Décembre.

DAUMAS Maurice (sous la direction)
1996 *Histoire Générale des techniques*, Editions des PUF, Paris.
1. Des origines au XVe siècle (1962).
2. Les premières étapes du machinisme XVe-XVIIIe siècle. (1964).
3. L'expansion du machinisme 1725-1860. (1968).
4. Les techniques de la civilisation industrielle : énergie et matériaux. (1978).
5. Les techniques de la civilisation industrielle : transformation, communication, facteur humain. (1979).

DELAUNAY Quynh
1994 *Histoire de la machine à laver*, Editions des Presses Universitaires de Rennes, Rennes.

DELEUZE Gilles
1968 *Le Bergsonisme*, Editions des PUF, coll. SUP, Paris
1968 *Différence et répétition*, Editions des PUF, Paris
1972 *L'Anti-œdipe*, Editions de Minuit, Paris.
1980 *Mille Plateaux*, Editions de Minuit, Paris.
1986 *Foucault*, Editions de Minuit, Paris.

DESCARTES
1966 *Le Discours de la Méthode*, [1636], Editions Garnier-Flammarion, Paris.

DESCOLA Philippe
1994 « Pourquoi les Indiens d'Amazonie n'ont-ils pas domestiqué le pécari ? Généalogie des objets et anthropologie de l'objectivation » in

Latour Bruno & Lemmonier Pierre. *De la préhistoire aux missiles balistiques,* Editions La Découverte, Paris.

DESCOLA, Philippe ; LENCLUD Gérard ; SEVERI Carlo ; TAYLOR Anne-Christine,
1988 *Les idées de l'anthropologie*, Editions Armand Colin, Paris.

DIAMOND Jared,
2000 *De l'inégalité parmi les sociétés. Essai sur l'homme et l'environnement dans l'histoire*, Editions Gallimard, coll. essai, Paris.

DIGARD Jean-Pierre
1979 « La technologie, nouveau souffle ou fin de parcours ?» in *L'Homme*, 19, Paris.
1987, « Jeux de structures. Segmentarité et pouvoir chez les nomades Baxtyari d'Iran », in *L'Homme*, 102, XXVII, (2), Paris.
1990 *L'homme et les animaux domestiques*, Editions Fayard, Paris.

DUMONT Louis
1966 *Homo Hiérarchicus. Le système des castes et ses implications*, Editions Gallimard, coll. Tel, Paris.
1983 *Essais sur l'individualisme*, Editions du Seuil, Paris.

DUPONT Jean-Claude et SCHMITT Stéphane
2004 *Une histoire de l'embryologie moderne (fin XVIIIe/XXe siècle). Du feuillet au gène.* Editions des Presses de l'Ecole Normale Supérieure, Paris.

DURKHEIM Emile
1986 *Les règles de méthode sociologique* (1937), Editions des PUF, Quadrige, Paris.

EDGERTON David
1998 « De l'innovation aux usages. Dix thèses éclectiques sur l'histoire des techniques », *Annales*, 4-5, p. 815-837.

ELLIOT SMITH Grafton
1927 «The diffusion of culture» in *Culture, the diffusion controversy*, Editions W. W Norton & Cie Inc., New York.
1929 *The migrations of early culture*, 1ère éd. 1915, Manchester University Press.

1933 *The diffusion of culture*, Editions Watts and Co, Londres.

EVANS-PRITCHARD Edward Evan
1974 *Les anthropologues face à l'histoire et à la religion*, [1962], Editions des P.U.F, Paris.

FIEDERMUTZ-LAUN Annemarie
2004 « Adolf Bastian, Robert Hartmann et Rudolf Virchow : médecins et fondateurs de l'ethnologie et de l'anthropologie allemandes » in *Quand Berlin pensait les peuples. Anthropologie, ethnologie et psychologie (1850-1890)*, Sous la direction de Céline Trautmann-Waller, Editions du CNRS, Paris

FINLEY Moses
1985 *L'invention de la politique*, Editions Champs Flammarion, Paris.

FORBES Robert James
1993   *Studies in ancient technology*, vol.2. (1958), Editions E-J. Brill, 3e edition, Leiden.

FOUCAULT Michel
1984 *L'usage des plaisirs*, Editions Gallimard, Paris.
1984 *Le souci de soi*, Editions Gallimard, Paris.
1984 «Deux essais sur le pouvoir et le sujet» et «Entretien», in Dreyfus et Rabinow, *Michel Foucault, un parcours philosophique*, p. 297-346, Editions Gallimard, Paris.
1986 «Omnes et singulatim. Vers une critique de la raison politique», in *Le Débat*, n°41 (sept.-nov.), Editions Gallimard, Paris.

FRIEDMANN Georges
1966 *Sept études sur la technique*, Editions Gonthier, Paris.

FROBENIUS Léo
1934 *La cultura como ser viviente : contornos de una doctrina cultural y psicologica*, Editions Espasa-Calpe SA, Madrid.
1952 *Histoire de la civilisation africaine*, [1933], Editions Gallimard (3ème éd.), Paris.

GAZAGNADOU Didier
2017 *The Diffusion of a Postal Relay System in Premodern Eurasia*, Kimé, Paris.

2013 *La poste à relais en Eurasie. La diffusion d'une technique d'information et de pouvoir. Chine – Iran – Syrie - Italie*, Editions Kimé, Paris.

1991 *Joseph Needham, un taoïste d'honneur* Editions du Félin, Paris.

1994 *La poste à relais. La diffusion d'une technique de pouvoir à travers l'Eurasie, Chine-Islam-Europe*, Editions Kimé, Paris.

1986a «L'origine du mot arabe funduq», *Studia Islamica*, n°64, Paris.

1986b *«L'origine d'une pratique de chancellerie mamelouke : la turra»*, *Studia Islamica*, n°64, Paris.

1987 «La lettre du gouverneur de Karak : relations entre Mamelouk et Mongols au XIIIe siècle», *Etudes Mongoles et Sibériennes*, n°18, Nanterre.

1989a «L'origine du "Lion passant à gauche" du sultan Baybars al-bunduqdari», *Der Islam*, n° 66.

1989b «Note sur le Tâlî kitâb wafayât al-'ayân d'Ibn al-Suqâ'î : une précieuse source quant aux relations mameluko-mongoles au XIIIe siècle», *Der Islam*, n°66.

1992 «D'une technique nomade à une pratique bureaucratique : la damga/tamga des turcs et des mongols», *Toplumbilim*, n°1, Istanbul.

1999a «Le chariot à main iranien (*gâri-yé dasti*). Modes de transport, rationalité technique et logique d'Etat», *Techniques et culture*, n°33, Janvier-Juin, Paris.

1999b «L'ordinateur américain et la chaise de coiffeur persane», in *Carrières d'objets*, Ch. Bromberger & D. Chevallier (éds), Editions du Patrimoine Ethnologique et de la Maison des Sciences de l'Homme, Paris.

2001a «Les étriers : contribution à l'étude de leur diffusion d'Asie vers les mondes iranien et arabe», *Techniques et culture*, n°37, juin, Paris.

2001b «Un savant chinois en terre d'Islam : à propos de la rencontre du philosophe et médecin Râzi et d'un lettré chinois», in *L'Orient au cœur; Mélanges en l'Honneur d'André Miquel*, Editions Maisonneuve et Larose, Paris.

2001c « Yâm » in Vol. XI. *Encyclopédie de l'Islam*, 2ème édition, Editions E-J Brill, Leyden.

2006 «Diffusion of Cultural Models, Body Transformation and Technology in Iran », in *Anthropology of the Middle East*, volume 1, Issue 1, a Berghahn Journal, New York-Oxford.

2007 « L'introduction tardive du diable et de la brouette au Moyen-

Orient (Iran et Egypte): un problème pour l'anthropologie des diffusions», in *Techniques et culture*, n°48-49..

GERNET Jacques
1956 *Les aspects économiques du bouddhisme dans la Chine du Ve au Xe siècle*, Publication de l'Ecole Française d'Extrême-Orient, Paris.
2000 *Le monde chinois*, Editions A. Colin, Paris. 2000.
1994 *L'intelligence de la Chine*, Editions Gallimard, Paris.

GILLE Bertrand
1978 *Histoire des techniques*, Editions Gallimard, Bibliothèque de La Pléiade, Paris.
1983 «Petites questions et grands problèmes : la brouette», in *La Recherche en Histoire des Sciences*, Editions du Seuil, coll. Point sciences, Paris

GODELIER Maurice
1996 *La production des grands hommes*, Editions Flammarion, coll. Champs Paris.
1973 *Horizon, trajets marxistes en anthropologie I*, nouvelle édition, Editions François Maspero, Paris.
1977 *Horizon, trajets marxistes en anthropologie II*, nouvelle édition, Editions François Maspero, Paris.
1978 «Préface » (p. 13-142), in *Sur les sociétés précapitalistes*, Centre d'Etudes et de Recherches Marxistes (C.E.R.M), Editions Sociales, Paris.

GOLDENWEISER Alexander
1927 «The diffusion controversy», in *Culture, the diffusion controversy*, Editions Norton & Cie Inc, New York.
1937 *Anthropology, an introduction to primitive culture*, Editions F.S. Crofts and Co., New York.

GOODY Jack
1999 *L'Orient dans l'Occident*, Editions du Seuil, coll. La librairie du XXe siècle, Paris.
1979 *La raison graphique*, la domestication de la pensée sauvage, Editions de Minuit, Paris.

GRAS Alain
2003 *Fragilité de la puissance. Se libérer de l'emprise technologique*,

Editions Fayard, Paris.
1997 «La technique, le milieu et la question du progrès : hypothèses sur un non-sens», in *Revue Européenne des Sciences Sociales*, tome XXXV, n°108, Paris.
1993 *Grandeur et dépendance : Sociologie des macro-systèmes techniques*, Editions des PUF, Paris.

GRATALOUP Christian
1996 *Lieux d'Histoire. Essai de géohistoire systématique*, Editions GIP Reclus, Montpellier.

GROSRICHARD Alain
1979 *Structure du sérail, la fonction du despotisme dans l'Occident classique*, Editions du Seuil, Paris.

GUILAINE Jean
2000 *Premiers paysans du monde. Naissances des agricultures*, Editions Errance, Paris.

HABERMAS Jurgen
1973 *La science et la technique comme "idéologie"*, Editions Gallimard, coll. Tel, Paris.

HAFEZ-E ABRU
1993 *Zubdat al-Tavârîkh*, (Hâj Saîd Djavâdî éditeur), Editions du Ministère de la culture et de la guidance islamique, 1372 H, Téhéran.

HALL Bert. S
1982 «Production et diffusion de certains traités de techniques au Moyen Age», in *Les arts mécaniques au Moyen âge*, in *Cahiers d'Etudes Médiévales*, 7, Editions Bellarmin et J. Vrin, Montréal-Paris.

HAUDRICOURT André Georges
1987 *La technologie, science humaine, Recherches d'histoire et d'ethnologie des techniques*, Editions de la Maison des Sciences de l'Homme, Paris.
1987 « La fonte en Chine, comment la connaissance de la fonte de fer a pu venir de la Chine à l'Europe médiévale » (1952) in *La technologie, science humaine*, Editions de la Maison des Sciences de l'Homme, Paris.

1986 *L'homme et la charrue à travers le monde* (avec M. J.-B. Delamarre), Editions La Manufacture, Paris.

HEGEL
1990 *Leçons sur l'histoire de la philosophie I et II*, (trad. 1954) Editions Gallimard, coll. Folio essais, trad. J. Gibelin, Paris.
1963 *Leçons sur la philosophie de l'Histoire*, Editions J. Vrin, Paris.

HERDER Johann G
1991 *Idées sur la philosophie de l'histoire de l'humanité*, [1784-1791], Editions Presses Pocket, Paris.

HERRENSCHMIDT Clarisse
2007 *Les trois écritures. Langue, nombre, code,* Editions Gallimard, Bibliothèques des sciences humaines, Paris.

HERSKOVITS Melville Jean
1967 *Les bases de l'anthropologie culturelle*, [1955], Editions Payot, Paris.

HILL Donald R.
1997 «Technologie» in R. Rashed (sous la direction), *Histoire des sciences arabes, vol 3*, Editions du Seuil, Paris.

IBN KHALDUN
1980 *Le voyage d'Occident et d'Orient* (traduit de l'arabe par A.Cheddadi), Editions Sindbad, Paris.

JABARTI 'Abd al-Rahmân
1965 *'Ajâ'ib al-athâr fî al-tarâjim wa'l akhbâr.* vol. 4. Vol. Edition en 7 volumes (1958-1967), Le Caire.

JAMARD Jean-Luc
1993 *Anthropologies françaises en perspective*, Editions Kimé, Paris.

JOVEINY 'Ala al-dîn 'Ata malik
1912 *Târîkh-e Jahan Gushâ*, éd. Mirza Mohammad, Gibb Mémorial Series, part 1, vol. XVI, Londres.

KOSAMBI Damodar
1970 *Culture et civilisation de l'Inde ancienne*, Ed. François Maspero, Paris.

KOYRE Alexandre
1973 *Etudes d'histoire de la pensée scientifique*, Editions Gallimard, coll. Tel, Paris.
1971 « Les philosophes et la machine » (1948) in *Etudes d'histoire de la pensée philosophique*, Editions Gallimard, coll. Tel, Paris.

KRIEGER Alex D.
1961 «On being critical» in *A. L. Kroeber : A Memorial*, Editions The Kroeber Anthropological Society Papers, n°25, Berkeley.

KROEBER Alfred-Louis
1992 *The nature of culture*, [1952], The University of Chicago Press, Chicago.
1940 «Stimulus diffusion», in *American anthropologist*, vol. 42, n°1.

KUPER Adam
2000 *L'anthropologie britannique au XXe siècle* (traduit de l'anglais par Gérald Gaillard), Editions Karthala, Paris.

LATOUR Bruno et LEMONNIER Pierre (sous la direction)
1994 *De la préhistoire aux missiles balistiques. L'intelligence sociale des techniques*, Editions La Découverte, Paris.

LEBEDYNSKY Iaroslav
2003 *Les Nomades. Les peuples nomades de la steppe des origines aux invasions mongoles (Ixe siècle av. J.-C – XIIIe siècle apr. J.-C.)*, Editions Errance, Paris.

LEMONNIER Pierre
1983 «L'étude des systèmes techniques, une urgence en technologie culturelle», in *Techniques et culture*, 1 (janvier-juin), Paris.

LE ROY LADURIE Emmanuel
1978 «Un concept : l'unification microbienne du monde (XIVe-XVIIe siècle)» in *Le territoire de l'Historien II*, Editions Gallimard, Bibliothèque des idées, Paris.
1969 *Le paysans du Languedoc*, Editions Flammarion, Paris.

LEROI-GOURHAN André
1971 *L'homme et la matière* (1943), Editions Albin Michel, Paris.

1973  *Milieu et techniques* (1945), Editions Albin Michel, Paris.
1964 *Le geste et la parole 1, Technique et Langage,* Ed. Albin Michel, Paris.
1965 *Le geste et la parole 2, La Mémoire et les Rythmes,* Editions Albin Michel, Paris.

LEVI-STRAUSS Claude
1961 *Race et histoire*, Editions Gonthier Flammarion, Paris.
1962 *La pensée sauvage*, Editions Plon, Paris.
1958 *Anthropologie structurale I*, Editions Plon, Paris.
1973 *Anthropologie Structurale II*, Editions Plon, Paris.

LITTAUER M. A and CROUWEL J. H
1979 *Wheeled vehicles and ridden animals in the ancient near east*, Editions E. J Brill, Leiden-Koln.

LOMBARD Maurice
1971 *L'Islam dans sa première grandeur, Editions Flammarion, coll. Champs, Paris.*

LOWIE Robert
1971 *Histoire de l'ethnologie classique*, [1937], Editions Payot, Paris.
1936 *Manuel d'anthropologie sociale*, [1934], Editions Payot, Paris.

LYOTARD Jean-françois
1993 *Moralités postmodernes*, Editions Galilée, Paris;
1988 *Le postmoderne expliqué aux enfants*, Editions Galilée, Paris.
1983 *Le différend*, Editions de Minuit, Paris.

MARCO POLO
1982 *Le devisement du Monde. Le Livre des Merveilles*, 2 vol., Editions La Découverte, Paris.

MALINOWSKI Bronislaw
1927 «The life of culture», in *Culture:the diffusion controversy*, Editions W. W Norton & Cie Inc., New York.
1968 *Une théorie scientifique de la culture*, [1944], Editions François Maspero, coll. Points, Paris.
1970 *Les dynamiques de l'évolution culturelle*, [1961], Editions Payot, Paris.

MARCUSE Herbert
1968 *L'homme unidimensionnel* [1964], Editions de Minuit, coll.
Points, Paris.

MARX Karl
1968 *Principes d'une critique de l'économie politique, Oeuvres, Economie II*, Editions Gallimard, Bibliothèque de La Pléiade, Paris.
1964 *Lettres sur "Le Capital"*, Editions Sociales, Paris.
1978 *Textes de Marx*, in Centre d'Etudes et de Recherches Marxistes
(C.E.R.M), Editions Sociales, Paris.

MARX Leo & ROE SMITH Merritt (Editors)
1995 *Does Technology Drive History? The Dilemma of Technological
Determinism*, Edition The MIT Press, Cambridge, Massachusets.

MAUSS Marcel
1968-1974 Œuvres complètes, 1, 2, 3, Editions de Minuit, Paris.
1950 *Sociologie et anthropologie*, Editions Gallimard, coll. Quadrige, Paris.
1947 *Manuel d'ethnographie*, Editions Payot, coll. Petite bibliothèque
(1967), Paris.

MAZOYER Marcel et ROUDART Laurence.
1997 *Histoire des agricultures, Du néolithique à la crise contemporaine*, Editions du Seuil, Paris.

MEAD Margaret,
1977 *Du givre sur les ronces, autobiographie* (1972 éd.anglaise), Editions du Seuil, Paris.

MERCIER Paul
1966 *Histoire de l'anthropologie*, Editions des PUF, Paris.

METAILIE Georges
1995 « Lettrés jardiniers en Chine ancienne » in *JATBA*, nouvelle série,
37 (1), Paris.
1991 «Avant-Propos», in *Joseph Needham, Dialogue des Civilisations
Chine-Occident : Pour une histoire œcuménique des sciences,* (G. Métailié éd), Editions La Découverte, Paris.
1988 «Aperçu de l'histoire du vocabulaire de la botanique au Japon :
assimilation et dispersion» in *Transferts de vocabulaire dans les sci-*

*ences* (Sous la Dir. de P. Louis & J. Roger), Editions du CNRS, Paris. 1997 «Needham's vision of the encounter of China and Europe : The case of the history of Botany», *Congrès International d'Histoire des Sciences*, Liège 20-26 Juillet.

MIQUEL André
1967-1980 *La géographie humaine du monde musulman jusqu'au milieu du 11ème siècle*, 4 vol. Editions Mouton & EPHE, Paris.
1977 *L'Islam et sa civilisation*, Editions A. Colin, Paris.

MOHEBBI Parviz
1996, *Techniques et ressources en Iran (VIIe-XIXe siècles)*. Editions de l'Institut Français de Recherche en Iran, Téhéran.

MONTANDON Georges
1934 *L'Ologénèse humaine. Traité d'ethnologie culturelle*, Editions Payot, Paris.

MORGAN Henri Lewis
1971 *La société archaïque*, Editions Anthropos, Paris.

MOSCOVICI Serge
1968 *Essai sur l'histoire humaine de la nature,* Editions Flammarion, Paris.

MUMFORD Lewis
1950 *Techniques et civilisation*, Editions du Seuil, coll. Esprit, Paris.

NEEDHAM Joseph
1954 *Science and Civilisation in China, Introductory orientations*, Cambridge University Press, Cambridge.
1973 *La science chinoise et l'Occident*, Editions du Seuil, coll. Points, Paris.

NIEDERER Arnold
1987 « Tendances de la recherche folklorique dans les pays de langue allemande » in CHIVA & JEGGLE 1987.

PERRY W. James
1935 *The primordial ocean. An introductory contribution to social psychology*, Methuen & CO. LTD, London.

PITT-RIVERS A. L. F
1906 *The evolution of culture and other essays*, Clarendon Press, Oxford.

POIRIER Jean
1968 «Histoire de la pensée ethnologique» in *Ethnologie Générale* (3-179), Editions Gallimard, Bibliothèque La Pléiade, Paris.

RASHED Roshdi (sous la direction)
1998 *Histoire des sciences arabes*, 3 volumes, Editions du Seuil, Paris.
2003 « Interview » in *Islam & Science, Journal of Islamic Perspectives on Science*, vol.1, number 1. June, p. 153-160, Published by the Center for Islam and Science, Canada.

RASHED Roshdi & Vahebzadeh Bijan
1999 *Al-Khayyâm, mathématicien*, avec Editions de l'Unesco, Paris.

RASHID AL-DIN FAZOLLAH HAMADANI
1994 *Jâmi'al-tavârîkh*, 2 vol. Editions Alborz, 1373 H, Téhéran.

RATZEL Friedrich
1887 «La diffusion de l'arc et des flèches en Afrique», in *Extrait des exposés de la classe de philologie et d'histoire de la Société Royale des Sciences de Saxe*, Séance du 14 mai.
1896 *The history of mankind*, Editions Macmillan and Co. Ltd, Londres.
1897 *Géographie politique*, Editions Economica (1988), Paris.

REICHHOLF Josef
1991 *L'émergence de l'homme*, Editions Champs Flammarion, Paris.
1994 *Mouvement animal et évolution*, Editions Flammarion, Paris.

RENOU Louis
1981 *La civilisation de l'Inde ancienne*, Editions Flammarion, coll. Champs, Paris.

RIVERS William, H. R
1914 *The history of the Melanesian society II*, Cambridge university press, Cambridge.

RIVET Paul
1924 «L'origine de l'industrie de l'or en Amérique», in *Der Welt-in-*

*dische Gids's Gravenhague*, n°8, Déc. 1924.
1929 *Sumérien et Océanien*, Editions E. Champion, coll. linguistique, Paris.
1929 «L'étude des civilisations matérielles, ethnographie, archéologie, préhistoire», in *Documents, Archéologie, Beaux-Arts, Ethnographie*, n°3, 1ère année, Paris.
1939 «L'origine des hommes et des techniques» (2ème éd.), *Conférences à l'Institut Supérieur Ouvrier*, Paris.

ROCHARD Philippe
2000 *Le « sport antique » du zurkhâne de Téhéran. Formes et significations d'une pratique contemporaine*. Thèse de doctorat. Université d'Aix-Marseille I, Université de Provence.

RODINSON Maxime
1968 *Islam et capitalisme*, Editions du Seuil, Paris.

RUPP-EISENREICH Brigitte
1991 « Diffusionnisme » in *Dictionnaire de l'ethnologie et de l'anthropologie* (sous la direction de P. Bonte et M. Izard), PUF, Paris.

SAKHARA Messaouda
2004 *Les Ryads, Maisons d'hôte de Marrakech. Approche anthropologique du phénomène des Ryads*. Mémoire de Maîtrise. Université Paris VIII.

SAPIR Edward
1967 *Anthropologie*, [1949], Editions du Seuil, coll. Points, Paris.

SAUVAGET Jean
1941 *La poste aux chevaux dans l'empire des Mamelouks*, Editions A. Maisonneuve, Paris.

SCHMIDT Wilhelm
1931 *Origine et évolution de la religion, les théories et les faits*, Editions B. Grasset, Paris.

SIGAUT François
1987 "Renouer le fil", in *Techniques et culture*, n°9, janvier-juin, Paris.
1985 "Ethnoscience et Technologie : les tâches de la technologie. Un

exemple, l'identification des formes de consommation des céréales" in *Techniques et culture*, n°5, janvier-juin, Paris.

SILVERSTEIN Adam
2007 *Postal systems in the Premodern Islamic World*, Cambridge University Press, Cambridge.

STOCKING Jr. George W.
1996 *After Tylor. British Social Anthropology 1888-1951*, The Athlone Press, London.
1974 *A Franz Boas Reader. The shaping of American anthropology 1883-1911*, Edited by George W. Stocking, Jr. Editions Midway reprint, University of Chicago Press, Chicago.

SWART Sandra
2003 «Riding high-horses, power and settler society, 1654-1840" in *Kronos*, vol.29, Environmental History, Special Issue, nov.1-28.

TARDE Gabriel
1993 *Les lois de l'imitation*, [1895], Editions Kimé, Paris.

TAYLOR Anne-Christine
1992 «L'évolutionnisme», in *Dictionnaire de l'Ethnologie et de l'Anthropologie*, P. Bonte, P & M. Izard (sous la direction), Editions des PUF, Paris.

TOCQUEVILLE Alexis de
1998 *Quinze jours dans le désert américain* (1860), Editions des Mille et une nuits, Paris.

TYLOR Edward Burnett
1865 *Researches in early history of mankind and the development of civilization*, Editions John Murray, Londres.
1876 *La civilisation primitive*, 2 vol. (trad. franç. Mme .P. Brunet de Primitive culture. Researches into the devlopment of mythology, philosophy, religion, language, art and custom), Editions Reinwald et Cie, Paris.

TRAUTMAN-WALLER Céline
2004 "introduction" in *Quand Berlin pensait les peuples. Anthropolo-*

*gie, ethnologie et psychologie (1850-1890)*, Editions du CNRS, Paris.

UMARI Shihab al-Dîn al-
1988 *al-ta'rîf bi'l mustalah al-sharîf*, Muhammad Husayn Shams al-Dîn éditeur, Editions Dâr al-kutub al-'ilmiya, Beyrouth.

VAN DER LEEUW Sander. E
1994a «La dynamique des innovations», in *Alliage, culture-science-technique*, n°20-21, automne-hiver, Paris.
1994b «Innovation et tradition chez les potiers mexicains ou comment les gestes techniques traduisent les dynamiques d'une société», in B. Latour & P. Lemonnier, *De la Préhistoire aux missiles balistiques*, Editions La Découverte, Paris.

VERNANT Jean-Pierre
1987 « l'individu dans la cité » in *Sur l'individu*, Editions du Seuil, Paris.

VEYNE Paul
1987 « L'individu atteint au cœur par la puissance publique » in *Sur l'individu*, Editions du Seuil, Paris.

VIALOU Denis
1996 *Au cœur de la Préhistoire. Chasseurs et artistes*, Editions Découvertes Gallimard, Paris.

VIGNE Jean-Denis,
2004 *Les débuts de l'élevage*, Editions Le Pommier & Cité des sciences et de l'industrie, Paris.

VIRILIO Paul
1977 *Vitesse et politique*, Editions Galilée, Paris.
1993 *L'art du moteur*, Editions Galilée, Paris.

WARNIER Jean-Paul
1999 *La mondialisation de la culture*, Editions La Découverte, coll. Repères, Paris.

WEBER Max
1991 *Histoire économique*, Editions Gallimard, Paris.

WHITE Leslie A.
1945 Diffusion vs. Evolution: an anti-evolutionnist fallacy» in *American Anthropologist*, vol. 47, n° 3, July September.
1959 *The evolution of culture*, Editions Mc Graw-Hill book cie, New York

WIET Gaston
1962 «Le monde musulman» in *Les origines de la civilisation technique*, tome I, (sous la direction de Maurice Daumas), Editions des PUF, coll. Quadrige [1996], Paris.

WHITE Lynn Jr.
1969 « Etrier, combat à cheval et féodalité » in *Technologie médiévale et transformations sociales* (1962), Editions de l'EHESS/Mouton, Paris.

WHITEHEAD Alfred Nortop
1969 *Les fonctions de la raison*, Editions Payot, Paris.

WISSLER Clark
1923 *Man and culture*, Editions Thomas Y. Crowell Cie, New-York.
1969 *Histoire des indiens d'Amérique du Nord,* [1940], Editions Robert Laffont, Paris.

ZURNDORFER Harriet. T.
1989 *Change and continuity in Chinese local history* (*the development of Hui-chen Prefecture 800 to 1800*), Editions E.J Brill, Leyden.
1981 « Chinese merchants and commerce in sixteenth century China » in *Leyden Studies in Sinology*, Editions E.J. Brill, Leyden.

# TABLE OF CONTENTS

Achevé d'imprimer
par Créaprojet en décembre 2016
Numéro d'impression : 611391
Imprimé en France

L'Imprimerie est titulaire de la marque Imprim'Vert®